HITLER'S
CROSS

The revealing story of how the
Cross of Christ was used as
a symbol of the Nazi agenda

HITLER'S CROSS

ERWIN W. LUTZER

MOODY PUBLISHERS
CHICAGO

All Scripture quotations, unless indicated, are taken from the *New American Standard Bible,* © 1960, 1962, 1963, 1968, 1971, 1972, 1973, 1975, and 1977 by The Lockman Foundation, and are used by permission.

ISBN: 0-8024-3583-1
ISBN-13: 978-0-8024-3583-5

We hope you enjoy this book from Moody Publishers. Our goal is to provide high-quality, thought-provoking books and products that connect truth to your real needs and challenges. For more information on other books and products written and produced from a biblical perspective, go to www.moodypublishers.com or write to:

Moody Publishers
820 N. LaSalle Boulevard
Chicago, IL 60610

9 10

Printed in the United States of America

*With affection to the members and friends of the Moody Church,
whose love and prayers have been a constant encouragement
to me and my family and whose witness for Christ is a reminder
that the Cross is still "the power of God unto salvation."*

CONTENTS

FOREWORD

This is a book that needed to be written.

Four years ago I experienced a defining moment on a bone-chilling day in the concentration camps of Auschwitz and Birkenau. The physical discomfort of the elements paled to insignificance when I walked through the rooms of this human hell that had witnessed spectacle after spectacle of the depths to which the human mind can descend once the conscience dies. Hitler himself said it all: "I want to raise a generation of young people devoid of a conscience—imperious, relentless, and cruel."

Speechless, I stared at the pictures of children hurt and humiliated by experimentations performed on them. I suddenly realized that everyone had left the room except for one other man who, like me, seemed overwhelmed and needed to say something to somebody. He turned and asked what kind of work I did.

I replied, "I am a minister of the gospel."

His reply carried the weight of history: "Gives you a lot to think about, doesn't it?" His implication was clear—where was the church in all this? I paused and then asked him what kind of work he did.

He hesitated, then said, "I am a judge from the state of New York."

"I think we *both* have a lot to think about," I said.

Much has been written about the Nazi era, but I have often wished that someone with insight and ability would help us achieve a deeper understanding of that dreadful period of history. We have needed a probing analysis that would do justice to what happened and relate it to the mind-set of every major institution in the land—even the church—and society at large.

This is that book. Erwin Lutzer brings a studied, yet passionate, response to the "hows" and "whys" and "what ifs" of this tragedy.

Here we have a biblical interpretation of how Adolf Hitler provoked the bloodiest, most unnecessary, most disruptive war in history and possibly changed irremediably the pattern of our world.

Scores have asked the obvious: "How could ordinary human beings wittingly or otherwise become pawns in Hitler's hands to discharge the most brutal orders?" Leading Nazi hunter, Peter Malkin, told of his experience while tracking down Adolf Eichmann. He confessed that he was shocked when he cupped his hand over Eichmann's mouth and realized that he was a mere human. The more he stared at him, the more he wondered how such a fragile man had wielded such devilish powers. Further, and more to the point, Malkin said, "I longed to get into his head and ask why, but I couldn't succeed."

In a recent article in the *Journal of Modern History,* Professor Michael R. Marrus of the University of Toronto attempts to unravel the mystery of Nazism in an essay entitled "Reflections on the Historiography of the Holocaust." As brilliant as his attempt is, here again a deep puzzlement remains. Quoting noted Holocaust historian Christopher Browning, who insisted that there was more to it than fanatical obedience, he writes, "These men seem to have been totally enthralled by their status as civil servants,'" and "whatever else they may have felt or desired personally, any action that might have tarnished their reputation as efficient and reliable bureaucrats was unthinkable to them. They were dominated by an internal compulsion to keep their records unstained. This compulsion was so strong that it blotted out any sense of individual responsibility." Marrus adds, "These men and men like them became desk murderers."

Such explanations leave us unsatisfied. Can we get behind all of the predictable analyzing and cut through to the reality of what it was all about? Can we get past the bureaucratic desks to learn from history and not repeat its mistakes?

That is why this treatment by Erwin Lutzer is so important for this generation. Once you begin this book it will be difficult for you to put it down. It is worthy of the most serious mind and eager intellect. What these pages unfold can make a difference in everyone who cares to conserve the future by remembering the past. In fact, if I recall correctly, that very challenge is etched on the walls of the Holocaust Museum in Jerusalem. Erwin Lutzer's book provides just such an impetus and, in so doing, serves mankind in a monumental sense.

RAVI ZACHARIAS

INTRODUCTION

W hile walking in the rain in Berlin recently, I thought I was going to have to abandon my search for the Bendlerblock Building that housed Hitler's War Ministry during the Nazi era. My map told me that the street I wanted was no longer called *Bendlerstrasse* but had been renamed *Stauffenbergstrasse* in memory of the man who had the courage to attempt to assassinate Hitler. I knew that in the courtyard of this building he, along with a half dozen others who participated in the failed plot, had been mercilessly shot. Their brutal murders had been put on film to satisfy the sadistic delight of the Führer. I wanted to stand where it had all happened and honor the heroism of these fallen men.

My sense of direction had been confused when I emerged from the subway, so I reluctantly concluded that I was walking in the wrong direction. But, as Providence would have it, I found the street and, with the guidance of a boy on a bicycle, was soon standing in the courtyard next to a memorial to Stauffenberg and his colleagues.

What I did not know is that this former Army War Ministry Building now houses a museum to the Resistance, a tell-all account of dozens of courageous men such as Stauffenberg, Niemöller, and Bonhoeffer. Here was proof, if proof were needed, that not all those who lived in

Germany during the Third Reich supported Hitler. Some were early in their opposition; others saw him for what he was once the atrocities began. But more individuals than I realized had been willing to give their lives to stop him.

But the pictures that caught my attention were those of Protestant pastors and Catholic priests giving the Nazi salute. I was even more surprised at the pictures of swastika banners that adorned the Christian churches—*swastika banners with the cross of Christ in the center!*

Standing in that museum I determined to study how Hitler had captured the Christian church; I knew that 95 percent of the people in Germany were either Protestant or Catholic. Now I wanted to know why the Christians in Germany did not condemn Hitler with one single, unified, and courageous voice. I wondered why millions willingly took Hitler's *Hakenkreuz* (hooked or broken cross) and superimposed on it the cross of our crucified Redeemer. Only later would I understand the extent to which *this confusion of crosses beguiled the German church and invited the judgment of God.*

I left the museum and caught a cab to the Kaiser-Wilhelm Memorial Church that I had seen on previous visits to Germany. This time I looked at the frescoes, pictures, and historical reliefs with a new set of glasses. What clues were there in the history of Germany that prepared the country (and its churches) for such a mass seduction? Could it happen again? More to the point, is it happening now, even in America, albeit in a different way? What signs should have alerted the church to Hitler's real agenda?

That Hitler was a god no one can doubt. He was worshiped by millions and thought himself to be both infallible and invincible. He seduced the masses and believed he would rule the world. In the end he was found to be a lesser god whose fate is shared by all those who stand in opposition to the Almighty. And subsequent history will confirm that his cross must bow to that of Another.

Hitler, I believe, is a prototype of the Antichrist who will someday arise and perform economic and political wonders. He, too, will mesmerize millions and demand the worship of the world. He will be able to accomplish feats of conquest and control that Hitler could not have dreamed possible. As we move through this era, I will briefly point out some striking parallels between the two men.

The church has always been poised between two gods and two crosses. On the one side is our Lord and Savior Jesus Christ, who died on a Roman cross, executed for the sins of the world. On the other side are any number of lesser gods and with them other crosses—those promises of deliverance that offer a false salvation.

Yes, we also face the temptation of bowing before the temporal gods that entice us to combine Christ with other religions, Christ and a political agenda, Christ and worldly pursuits. The experience of the church in Nazi Germany reminds us that Christ must always stand alone; He must be worshiped not as One who stands alongside the governmental leaders of this world but as standing above them, *as King of kings and Lord of lords.*

Since I believe, as Santayana has said, that those who disregard history are condemned to repeat it, I believe we are derelict if we do not study the Nazi era to learn all we can for the church in the present day. And, as we shall see, in so doing we might also be preparing ourselves for our own impending future.

We will discover that the Nazi era shouts its lessons to the church of America. It warns us, challenges us, and forecasts what might happen in the days ahead. Whether we will heed its warnings, accept its challenges, and recognize its subtle deceptions is up to us.

With the Bible in one hand and the history books in the other, we begin our journey. When we are finished, we should be on our knees asking God to keep us faithful to the cross of Christ, no matter what the cost. And we should be the wiser for having identified the signposts that are leading our own country down what could be a similar path.

Let's begin.

CHAPTER ONE

WAITING FOR HITLER

udolf Hess, the son of a German wholesale merchant and student at the University of Munich, wrote a prize-winning essay answering the question: "What Kind of a Man Will Lead Germany Back to Her Previous Heights?" When he met Hitler in 1920, he was struck by the parallels between what he had written and the man who was now in his presence. Hitler was stirred by the essay and impressed with the man who had such uncanny insight. Little wonder they became close friends.

First and foremost, said Hess, this individual had to be a man of the people, a man whose roots were deeply embedded in the masses so that he would know how to treat them psychologically. Only such a man could gain the trust of the people; that, however, was only to be his public image.

Second, in reality such a man should have nothing in common with the masses; for when the need arose, he should not shrink from bloodshed. Great questions are always decided by "blood and iron." The public image must be kept separate from the actual performance.

Third, he had to be a man who was willing to trample on his closest friends to achieve his goals. He must be a man of terrible hardness; as the needs arise, he must crush people with the boots of a grenadier.[1]

Hitler vowed he would be that man. He would give the appearance of being one of the masses, but in reality he would be quite another. When brutality was called for, he could act with force and decisiveness. He would do what the individuals among the masses could not. He would not shrink from cruelty.

Privately Hitler prepared for war; publicly he gave speeches about his desire for peace. Privately he enjoyed pornography; publicly he insisted on right conduct, no swearing, no off-color jokes in his presence. At times he could be charming and forgiving; most other times he was monstrously cruel, as when he insisted that those who conspired against him be "hung on a meat hook and slowly strangled to death with piano wire, the pressure being periodically released to intensify the death agonies." Privately (and sometimes publicly) he prided himself in his honesty, yet often he reveled in his ability to deceive. "The German people must be misled if the support of the masses is required," he mused.

Hitler engineered the atrocities seen in *Schindler's List,* a movie that dramatized but a small slice of "the final solution." He was a cauldron of contradictions. During his days in Vienna he saved dried bread to feed squirrels and birds and just months after coming to power signed three pieces of legislation to protect animals; yet he worked himself into a frenzy of delight over the pictures of great capitals in Europe in flames. He was especially ecstatic at the bombing of Warsaw and London and angry with the commandant of Paris for not setting that city on fire.

He could weep with tenderness when talking to children and rejoice over the completion of another concentration camp. Compassionate and even generous with family and friends, he would become filled with vindictive rage at anyone—including close friends—who stood in the way of his agenda. He could be charming or brutal, generous or savage. "He who spoke the words of Jesus," said Robert Waite, "hated all mankind."

Hitler holds a fascination for us because his dictatorship enjoyed such wide support of the people. Perhaps never in history was a dictator so well liked. He had the rare gift of motivating a nation to want to follow him. Communist leaders such as Lenin or Mao Tse-tung arose to power through revolutions that cost millions of lives; consequently, they were hated by the masses. Hitler attracted not only the support of the middle class but also of university students and professors. For example, psychologist Carl Jung grew intoxicated with "the mighty phenomenon of National Socialism at which the whole world gazes in astonishment."

Hitler arose in Germany at a time when the nation was a democracy. He attained his power legitimately, if unfairly. The nation was waiting for him, eager to accept a demagogue who appeared to have the talent needed to lead her out of the abyss. *The people yearned for a leader who would do for them what democracy could not.*

THE EARLY MIRACLES

Hitler's report card was filled with such astounding achievements that many Christians saw him as an answer to their prayers. Some Christians, I have been told—yes, I said Christians—took the picture of Christ from the wall in their homes and substituted a portrait of Hitler. Winston Churchill observed Hitler in 1937 and said that his accomplishments were "among the most remarkable in the whole history of the world." Here is a partial list of what he was able to do without the obstructions inherent in a democracy.

1. He revived a collapsed economy in five years.
2. He erased the shame of Germany's defeat in World War I by reclaiming the Rhineland and discarding the unfair Treaty of Versailles.
3. He gave millions of Germans attractive vacations through his *Kraft durch Freude* ("Strength through joy") program.
4. He established training schools for those who were unskilled and brought the nation to full employment.
5. He brought crime under control.
6. He built freeways and promised the production of a car that ordinary Germans would soon be able to afford.
7. He gave Germans a reason to believe in themselves, to believe that they could become great again.

If he had died before World War II, one historian mused, he would have gone down in history as "Adolf the Great, one of the outstanding figures in German history."

But Hitler didn't die before World War II; he didn't die until the German people had surrendered their personal rights, until laws were enacted that led to the extermination of more than 8 million people, and until Germany and several other countries were destroyed in a war that killed 50 million people in the greatest bloodbath in history. He didn't die until *thousands of pastors joined the SS troops in swearing personal allegiance to him.*

Of course the Germans did not know that it would turn out that way. But let's not overlook the fact that they wanted a dictatorship; they yearned for a strong leader who would bypass the slow pace of democratic reform. People were starving, political crimes were multiplying, and Germany found herself under a cloud of national shame. The democratic process was stalled with more than two dozen different parties vying for political power. Democracy might be preferable when times are good; a dictatorship works best when times are bad. For Germany the times were bad, very bad.

But we are still left with a nagging question: Why did the German people, and more particularly the church, not part ways with Hitler once his real agenda became known? We might understand their initial deception, but why did so many hundreds of thousands of Germans directly or indirectly participate in the atrocities that became so much a part of the Nazi agenda? These multiplied thousands of otherwise decent Germans boycotted Jewish businesses, participated in mock trials, and brutally controlled the prison camps. In short, Hitler had helpers, millions of helpers, who did his bidding no matter how despicable their assignments became.

Is it true, as some have suggested, that the Germans of Hitler's era were somehow half-man and half-demon, the likes of which will never appear on the earth again? Was historian Friedrich Meinecke correct when he suggested that the Nazis were a "fluke" or "accident" of history that will, in all probability, never recur? Or were the Germans not only human but fully human, simply human without the veneer, human without the constraints of society and God?

The answer, as we shall discover, is that the Germans of the Nazi era—indeed Hitler himself—were all too human. Just read today's headlines about Bosnia, the atrocities in Yugoslavia, or the strangulation of children in our neighborhoods, and it becomes clear that raw humanity is not very pretty. Evil held in check often erupts when the conditions are right. When the restraints are gone, when people are desperate, and when power is up for grabs, the human heart is laid bare for all to see. *We are naive if we think Nazi Germany cannot happen again. In fact, the Bible predicts that it will.*

THE CONFLICT OF CHURCH AND STATE

The story of how Hitler crushed the church in Germany is, of course, the primary focus of this book. In passing, we should note that he banned prayer in schools, changed Christian holidays into pagan festivals, and eventually forced the church leadership to accept his outrageous demands. His political machine swallowed the church whole because the church had lost its biblical mission. Thus the state not only interfered with religious practices but controlled them. A powerful state has always been a threat to the existence and influence of the church. Whether the threat be Nazism, Communism, or humanism, *a state that is hostile to religion will always attempt to push the church toward forced irrelevancy.*

Even without a dictatorship a state can marginalize the influence of the church. As the state expands its powers, it can initiate laws that limit the church's freedoms. Consider the phrase "the separation of church and state." Interpreted in one way, it can mean that the church should be free to exercise its influence and practice religion without interference from the state. That kind of separation is exactly what the church in Germany so desperately needed.

However, here in America the phrase "separation of church and state" is given a sinister twist by civil libertarians. To them it means that religious people should not be allowed to practice their religion in the realm that belongs to the state. Religion, we are told, should be practiced privately; the state must be "cleansed" from every vestige of religious influence. By insisting that the state be "free for all religions," organizations such as the ACLU in effect makes it free for none!

Here in America, where church and state are separate, our conflict is quite different from the predicament of the church in Nazi Germany, where religion and politics had always been wedded in a close, if stormy, marriage. Yet this study of Germany will force us to grapple with the same questions the German people faced half a century ago.

- What is the responsibility of the church when the state adopts unjust policies?

- For Christians, where does patriotism end and civil disobedience begin?
- Is silence in the face of injustice the same as complicity? Are small compromises justified if they might prevent the state from crushing religious freedom?
- How can the church effectively spread the gospel while fighting an unpopular battle for social justice?
- What warning signs are there when the church buys into the culture of the day and can no longer stand against prevalent evils?
- What is the relationship between a church's theology and its ability to withstand the crushing power of the secular state?

The answers to these questions are not easy. Whether in Europe or America, tension has always existed between church and state. To appreciate the struggle in the Third Reich, we must understand the history of the First and Second Reichs, where the seeds of the church's deception were planted. And the Third Reich will help us to understand a coming Fourth Reich that will dwarf Hitler for the magnitude of its scope and cruelty.

That word *reich* is best translated as "empire" or "kingdom." To the German ear it almost has a sacred tone. How well I remember my parents, German-speaking people who emigrated to Canada, teaching us the Lord's Prayer: *Dein Reich komme, dein Wille geschehe . . .* For the Nazis that word *reich* would come to express the mystical and eternal German kingdom.

Join me as we take a quick tour of the relationship between the church and reich in European history.

THE FIRST REICH (800–1806)

Charlemagne (Charles the Great) was crowned emperor by Pope Leo III on Christmas Day in the year 800. Charlemagne was praying in front of a crypt in Saint Peter's Basilica in Rome while Leo sang the Mass. Then without warning, Leo placed the crown on Charles's head as the congregation gave its blessing. Charles was both surprised and pleased; he left St. Peter's determined to use the sword to build the one universal, Catholic church. His conquests brought unity to Europe and began the Holy Roman Empire (an empire that Voltaire said was neither holy, nor Roman, nor an empire).

Nevertheless, Charlemagne cemented the growing unity of church and state that was begun during the days of Constantine (274–337). During the first two centuries A.D., the church was persecuted by the Roman Empire; when Constantine conquered the city of Rome in 312, the church married its enemy and became corrupted by it. The sword of steel (the state) would now exist to promote the sword of Scripture (the church). The coronation of Charles the Great was the high point of the fatal marriage.

Though Charles had mistresses and a limited education, he saw his role as the protector of the doctrines of the church. Since infant baptism was the law of the land, anyone who was baptized as an adult upon profession of faith in Christ was persecuted and even put to death. It was not that Charles was interested in theology; rather, he believed that the universal church had to remain universal, encompassing everyone within the boundaries of the empire. Religion unified the diverse countries, and infant baptism would keep future generations "Christian."

THE NAZIS WRAPPED THE CROSS IN THE SWASTIKA, MAKING THE CROSS A WEAPON TO FURTHER HITLER'S AGENDA.

Of course the state also persecuted those who differed in their interpretation of the Mass and those who spurned the authority of the pope. Such "heretics" were tried, imprisoned, or even put to death. Interestingly, many true believers claimed that little changed when the Roman Empire was "christianized." Previously, they were persecuted by pagan Rome; next they were persecuted by religious Rome. Either way, the sword hurt just as much!

This uneasy relationship between church and state (sometimes cozy, sometimes competitive, and often corrupt) did not end with the Reformation of 1517. Even today the church in Europe (both Catholic and Protestant) is supported through taxes. Of course the so-called golden rule often applies: Whoever has the gold has the rule! In my opinion, the marriage of church and state is always detrimental to the mission of the church. Either the church will change its message to accommodate the state's political agenda, or the political rulers will use the church to their own ends. Regardless, the purity of the church is compromised.

This unholy unity contributed to the paralysis of the church during the Hitler era. At the very moment it should have been condemning the politics of the day with one unified voice, the church found its existence dependent upon the goodwill of the state. The church had a history of allegiance to its militaristic Prussian heroes. In the fourth century Constantine had the cross of Christ emblazoned on the shields of his soldiers; in the twentieth century, the Nazis wrapped the Cross in the swastika, making the cross a weapon to further Hitler's agenda. But I'm ahead of the story.

To return to the history of the First Reich: From 1273 to 1806, the Holy Roman emperors were, for the most part, Germans from Austria, known as the Habsburg dynasty. The conflict between church and state continued until the last centuries of the empire when the emperors lost much of their power and rival kingdoms arose throughout Europe.

Where does Germany fit into all of this? During the sixteenth and seventeenth centuries, the territory of Brandenburg/Prussia arose and was ruled by a succession of powerful kings. The Brandenburg Gate in the heart of Berlin was built in honor of the territory that bears its name. The beautiful palaces of the Prussian kings can still be admired today on the outskirts of Berlin. Prussia, as we will learn, became involved in a series of wars and eventually brought unity to the German-speaking people of Europe.

In 1804, the pope tried to crown Napoleon Bonaparte in the Notre Dame Cathedral in Paris, but Napoleon snatched the crown from the pontiff and crowned himself, signifying that, unlike Charlemagne, he had won the right to be emperor on his own merits! Napoleon's goal was to substitute a French empire for the German one that had dominated Europe for so many centuries. After crushing Austria, he turned on Prussia; and when he marched victoriously into Berlin, the First Reich had come to its end.

However, after Napoleon's defeat at Waterloo, the state of Prussia was re-created, and French dominance soon ended. In fact, Prussia rebounded from French rule with a deepened sense of nationalism and, through a series of wars, unified Germany. Thus the conditions were right to inaugurate a Second Reich.

THE SECOND REICH (1871–1918)

Picture Germany as a collection of about three hundred independent states, each having its own organization, often its own currency, and even separate weights and measures. What might be done to bring unity to the fragmented German states?

Otto von Bismarck (1815–1898), the shrewd new premier of Prussia, had the political savvy to know that only war could unify the German-speaking peoples of Europe. He reversed the defeat suffered under Napoleon and prepared a powerful army. The consummate politician, he provoked a war with Austria, bringing that country under Prussian control. Next, he lured France into battle, turning the tables on the very country that had defeated Prussia under Napoleon's able leadership. Germany at last was unified—and powerful!

To add insult to France's defeat, Bismarck had Prussian King William I brought to France to be crowned in the Hall of Mirrors in Versailles as the head of a new, unified empire. He was crowned Kaiser (Caesar) Wilhelm, sending a clear message that his agenda was to reclaim every country that once belonged to the old Holy Roman Empire and bring it under German rule. Thus the Second Reich had an auspicious beginning.

If the First Reich prepared the way for Hitler by unifying church and state, the Second Reich contributed to the paralysis of the church by teaching that there must be a split between private and public morality. Bismarck claimed to have had a conversion experience to Christianity while visiting in the home of some pietistic friends. But he was faced with the realization that as a political statesman he had to violate the moral principles that governed his private behavior as a Christian. He reasoned that when acting as a servant of the state, a man was not bound by the same morality he should have as an individual. *The state, it was argued, should not be judged according to conventional law because its responsibilities went beyond ordinary human values.*

This dichotomy—which some would say goes back to Luther, who insisted that the peasants obey their leaders no matter how tyrannical—was taught in the German churches. Paul's teaching that we should be subject to political authorities was emphasized (Romans 13:1–2). The laws of the state were to be obeyed without asking for a moral rationale for what one was commanded to do.

As Bismarck said, "I believe I am obeying God when I serve my king." A commitment to high national honor was a sacred duty.

Those who participated in the atrocities of the Third Reich frequently appealed to this distinction to defend their actions. When asked how they could reconcile their brutality with their humanistic values, they often replied, "Well, that was war, and obviously one has to do his duty, no matter how hard." In the words of the notorious Eichmann, "I had to obey the laws of my country and my flag."

Bismarck agreed with his Prussian predecessor Frederick the Great, who once boasted that "salvation is God's affair; everything else belongs to me!" This double standard became known as the doctrine of the "two spheres," a subject to which we shall return when we discuss the role of the church in Nazi Germany. That doctrine is still found among politicians today who say that privately they oppose abortion or the imposition of gay rights upon society, but they don't think that their private views should influence their input into public legislation.

Under Bismarck a *Reichstag* (German Parliament) was formed, and Bismarck was named prime minister and later chancellor. Though a new constitution was written, the Parliament had practically no power but was merely a forum for the discussion and debate of political issues. Both Bismarck and the Kaiser shared a contempt for individual freedom and democracy. Only a monarchy, they believed, could deal with all the problems of a loosely knit Germany that needed to be kept in line. Bismarck deeply believed the expression he coined on the day he was installed as prime minister: "The great questions of the day will not be settled by resolutions and majority votes . . . but by blood and iron."

In 1871, when Kaiser Wilhelm was coronated, he laid the cornerstone for the massive Reichstag in Berlin. If you have visited the city or seen pictures of the structure, you should be reminded that it stands as a monument to the Second Reich. In fact, now that Germany is unified, moves are underway to reinstate the German Parliament in the Reichstag building.

When World War I began in 1914, most Germans were hungry for war, believing that war was, in the words of Prussian General von Moltke, part of God's creation, "enfolding the noblest virtues of courage, self-renunciation, loyalty, and willingness to sacrifice with one's life." They also believed that the war that began in the summer would be won "before Christmas."

No one wanted war more than Adolf Hitler, who was twenty-five years old at the time. He volunteered for service and later reflected, "I am not ashamed to say that, overcome with rapturous enthusiasm, I fell to my knees and thanked Heaven from an overflowing heart for granting me the good fortune of being allowed to live at this time."[2]

Thanks to America's decision to enter the war, Germany surrendered on November 9, 1918. Kaiser Wilhelm II was humiliated and, to save his life, fled to the Netherlands, where he spent the rest of his days studying occult writings to try to understand why Germany had lost the war. After all, his soothsayers, including the famous Houston Chamberlain (whom we shall meet again in a future chapter), had assured him that the superior Germans were destined to win.

WHAT IS TAUGHT IN PHILOSOPHY CLASSROOMS TODAY IS BELIEVED BY THE MAN ON THE STREET TOMORROW.

When Hitler heard the news of Germany's defeat, while recuperating from an attack of mustard gas, he had a mystical vision that he believed was his "call" into politics. He cried for the first time since the death of his mother. He then knew he was destined to play a role in Germany's future. The world eventually would have to cope with the consequences of that decision.

With the defeat of Germany and the formation of a new constitutional government, the Second Reich had come to an inglorious end.

THE THIRD REICH (1933–1945)

Given a legacy of militarism—the exaltation of the state above ordinary morality—we can see that Germany was waiting for a dictator to lead her out of her humiliation. Let's trace the roots of the tree that bore such bitter fruit.

THE PHILOSOPHICAL ROOTS

Some people think that philosophers sit in ivory towers and spin theories that have little to do with the life of the ordinary, hardworking citizen. But in point of fact, philosophers have often ruled entire countries (Karl Marx is but one example). What is taught in philosophy classrooms today is believed by the man on the street tomorrow.

Germany has had its philosophers too, brilliant men who gained a wide audience through their teachings and writings. They prepared the soil and even planted the seeds of nationalism and fanned hatred of the Jews. Whether they knew it or not, they were preparing the way for Hitler. Let's meet just two of them.

Georg Hegel (1770–1831) held the chair of philosophy at the Berlin University. His dialectical philosophy, which inspired Marx, preached the glorification of the state, saying it was "God walking on earth." Individual rights, he believed, simply got in the way of the state as supreme authority. The state, he said, is "the moral universe . . . and has the foremost right against the individual, whose supreme duty is to be a member of the state . . . for the right of the world spirit is above all special privileges."[3]

War, Hegel taught, was the great purifier that was necessary for the ethical health of the people. As for private moral virtues such as humility and patience, these must never stand in the way of the state's agenda; indeed the state must crush such "innocent flowers." Here is the ultimate justification for the doctrine of the two spheres: Private morality should be private! State morality was something different altogether.

Hegel predicted that Germany would flourish again since she represented the highest form of dialectical development. Let the French do as they wish; let Russia and Britain grow strong, he said. The laws of history are on Germany's side. She deserves to rise again, and arise she will.

As might be expected, Hegel denied the uniqueness of Christianity and argued that the Old Testament had to be rejected because of its Jewish roots. A pure Christian faith could be had only by a pure race, namely the Germans. Thus, a new Christianity would have to evolve that was suited to the higher German spirit.

Friedrich Nietzsche (1844–1900), the son of a Lutheran pastor, wrote a bitter assault on Christianity, accusing it of weakness and of being the cause of Germany's ills. In his *Antichrist,* he wrote, "I call Christianity the one great curse, the one enormous and innermost perversion, the one moral blemish of mankind. . . . I regard Christianity as the most seductive lie that has yet existed."[4] Christianity, he said, with its emphasis on the virtues of mercy and forgiveness, made Germany weak.

Nietzsche, you will remember, proclaimed that God was dead. He wrote, "Do we not hear anything yet of the noise of the grave diggers who are burying God? Do we not smell anything yet of God's decomposition? Gods, too, decompose. God is dead and we have killed him." The churches, he said, were tombs and sepulchers of God.

Nietzsche faced the frightful implications of atheism without blinking. Listen to how he described what the death of God means for man: "How shall we, the murderers of all murderers comfort ourselves? . . . Who will wipe the blood off us? What water is there to clean ourselves? What festivals of atonement, what sacred games shall we have to invent? Is not the greatness of this deed too great for us? Must not we ourselves become gods simply to seem worthy of it?"[5]

Nietzsche knew that with God's death there was no answer for man's guilt, no one to wipe the blood from our hands. Since God was dead, a successor would have to be found. Nietzsche knew that in an atheistic state the strong would rule the weak. He proclaimed the coming of the master race and a superman who would unify Germany and perhaps the world. A coming elite would rule from which this superman would spring. He and those around him would become "lords of the earth." This man would be "the magnificent blond brute, avidly rampant for spoil and victory."

Nietzsche, who died in 1900, did not live to see the rise of the Third Reich or the spread of atheistic Communism. But his prediction that the twentieth century would be one of bloodshed was, unfortunately, all too true. With God out of the way, humans would be unrestrained; there would be no fear of judgment, no belief in the virtues of morality. When humans realized that history was based on raw power, there would be universal madness. (Note that Nietzsche himself was insane for the last eleven years of his life.) As Ravi Zacharias put it: Nietzsche understood that man "in stabbing at the heart of God, had in reality, bled himself."[6]

Nietzsche reinforced the prevailing philosophy in Germany that a genius was above the law, that he should not be bound by the morals of ordinary men. Private virtues simply stood in the way of the greater virtues of control and power. Compassion made a state weak; unbridled power made a state strong. It was not the meek but the ruthless who would inherit the earth. The superman would crush cherished virtues so that he could rule the world. Listen once more to these chilling words from Nietzsche's pen.

> The strong men, the masters, regain the pure consciousness of a beast of prey; monsters filled with joy, they can return from a fearful succession of murder, arson, rape, and torture with the same joy in their hearts. . . . To judge morality properly, it must be replaced by two concepts borrowed from zoology: the taming of the beast and the breeding of a specific species.[7]

Is it any wonder that Hitler was so mesmerized by Nietzsche that he gave a copy of his writings to his friend Benito Mussolini? Hitler often visited Nietzsche's museum in Weimar and posed for photographs of himself staring enraptured at the bust of that great man. Nietzsche, many historians believe, would have abhorred Hitler's excesses, particularly his anti-Semitism. Be that as it may, Hitler adopted him as a spiritual brother and interpreted his writings to suit his purposes. Whether justly or not, Nietzsche's writings were used, in the words of one historian, "to unleash all the devils of hell."

IT HAS BEEN SAID THAT AFTER GOD DIED IN THE NINETEENTH CENTURY, MAN DIED IN THE TWENTIETH. FOR WHEN GOD IS DEAD, MAN BECOMES AN UNTAMED BEAST.

Hitler considered himself the superman of Nietzsche's philosophy. He rejoiced that the doctrine of God that had always stood in the way of brutality and deceit had now been removed. Once man had replaced God, the way was clear for Nietzsche's superrace led by a superman to dominate the world.

Perhaps now we can better understand the concentration camps. Ideas do have consequences, and the notion that God was dead freed humans to do as they pleased. With God cast down, man was free to rise up and pursue his unrestrained lust for power.

Victor Frankl, who survived the Holocaust, wrote this stinging critique:

> The gas chambers of Auschwitz were the ultimate consequence of the theory that man is nothing but the product of heredity and environment—or, as the Nazis liked to say, "Of Blood and Soil." I'm absolutely convinced that the gas chambers of Auschwitz, Treblinka, and Maidanek were ultimately prepared not in some ministry or other in Berlin, but rather at the desks and in the lecture halls of nihilistic scientists and philosophers.[8]

It has been said that after God died in the nineteenth century, man died in the twentieth. For when God is dead, man becomes an untamed beast.

THEOLOGICAL ROOTS

Germany was (and still is) the hotbed of liberal scholarship that stripped Christianity of its uniqueness. An influential theologian named Ludwig Feuerbach would have agreed with the New Agers of today that the doctrine of God should be more properly interpreted as the doctrine of man. The Incarnation, he said, teaches us that the Being who was worshiped as God is now recognized as a man. Man must no longer be second in religion; he is first. According to Feuerbach, that man is God is the highest ethic and the turning point of world history. *If Christ was divine, it was only because all of us are.*

German scholars "demythologized" the New Testament, that is, stripped it of its myths so that a kernel of truth could be found. Some theologians openly stated that the miracles of the New Testament should be forgotten and the attention of the masses fixed on the miracle of the rise of Germany to its place of leadership in the world. Little wonder that they were willing to hide the cross of Christ within the swastika.

Along with the humanization of God came the deification of man. In Weimar, Goethe had eloquently argued that man must replace God as the center of art, philosophy, and history. As a child of the Enlightenment, he believed that religion had to be rethought and made to glorify man rather than God. He could never have dreamed, however, that in exalting man he was opening the door to unrestrained evil. It is not a historical accident that Buchenwald, one of the

Nazi concentration camps, was only six miles from Weimar, the seat of the Enlightenment. Hitler had, I am told, perverted delight in setting up a death camp near the city that prided itself in tolerance and the glory of man.

If, as Frankl said, the ovens of Auschwitz were prepared in the lecture halls of Europe, we can also say that those ovens were fueled by liberal scholarship that glorified man and declared God to be irrelevant. Such doctrines undercut the ability of the church to stand against the atrocities of the Third Reich. Substituting human ideas for the revelation of God, *the Third Reich reinterpreted the cross of Christ to advance a pagan agenda.*

POLITICAL ROOTS

Germany was badly stung by its defeat and humiliation after World War I. Political chaos was rampant throughout the major cities. In Munich, the Communist party, encouraged by the successful revolution in Russia in 1918, was attempting to seize control. Political organizations were forming both to the right and the left. In Berlin, riots and social instability forced the Parliament to leave the Reichstag and move to the National Theater in Weimar to form a new government based on democratic principles and ideals.

So it was that on November 9, 1918, the Republic was proclaimed. After six months of debate, a constitution was adopted that, on paper at least, appeared capable of bringing about a stable democracy. It incorporated ideas from England, France, and the United States. The people were made sovereign, and the constitution declared that "all Germans are equal before the law." The phrase "For the German People" was engraved on the Reichstag where it can still be seen today.

The attempt at democracy might have succeeded were it not for the Treaty of Versailles that had been drawn up by the Allies. It restored Alsace-Lorraine to France, and territories Bismarck had conquered to Belgium and Denmark and Poland. In addition, Germany had to make war reparation payments of 132 billion gold marks, or about $33 billion, a sum it could not possibly pay.

The treaty in effect disarmed Germany. It restricted the army to 100,000 men and prohibited it from having tanks or planes. The navy was reduced to little more than a token force. Then, in a final act of humiliation, Germany had to agree to take responsibility for having begun the war; and the treaty demanded that it turn Kaiser Wilhelm II over to the Allies along with eight hundred other war criminals.

Britain warned that if Germany did not sign the treaty, she would initiate a blockade around Germany and in effect starve out the Germans. The Allies were insisting on an immediate reply from Germany with the deadline set for June 24, 1919.

Finally, with the agreement of the provisional leader of the Republic, Field Marshal von Hindenburg, and with the approval of the National Assembly, the treaty was ratified. Four days later it was signed in the Hall of Mirrors in the palace at Versailles, the very place where the Second Reich had had its heady beginning when Kaiser Wilhelm I was crowned in 1871. Not only had Germany lost the war; she had also lost her dignity.

ECONOMIC ROOTS

The Republic, for all its good intentions, was now blamed for accepting the unfair terms of the treaty and for the subsequent economic crisis. The German mark, which had at one time been valued at 4 to a dollar, fell to 75 to a dollar, then 400 to the dollar. By 1923 it had fallen to 7,000 marks per dollar. When Germany defaulted on its war payments, the French president commanded his troops to occupy the Ruhr area. Thus the industrial heart of Germany was cut off from the rest of the country.

That act triggered the final strangulation of Germany's choking economy. Immediately after the action of the French in January of 1923, the mark plunged to 18,000 per dollar, and by November it took 4 billion marks to equal a dollar. In effect, the mark was canceled.

There is a story, perhaps fictitious, of a woman who filled her wheelbarrow with German marks and left them outside the store, confident that no one would bother stealing the money. Sure enough, when it was time to pay for her groceries, she walked outside only to discover that the bundles of money were left on the ground but the wheelbarrow was gone! We might smile at the story, but Germans found nothing to smile about. Their savings were totally wiped out. They had lost faith in their government. The people suffered immeasurably, and the worst was yet to come.

In 1923, Hitler's dramatic attempt to overthrow the Bavarian government failed (the Putsch that will be briefly described in the next chapter). He was convicted of treason; and after his incarceration in

Hitler leaving Landsberg Prison in 1924.

Landsberg Prison, he decided to gain power through the political process. *He would use democracy as the path to power, then crush that democracy once he gained control.*

The economic outlook improved in 1925–29 as unemployment decreased and retail sales went up. Ten years after the war had ended, the German Republic seemed to come into its own. The Nazi party was all but dead. But with the passion of world conquest burning in his breast, Hitler simply would not give up. He kept waiting, hoping that Germany would experience more bad times.

The worldwide depression of 1929 gave Hitler the opportunity he sought. Revolutionary that he was, he could thrive only in bad times, when unemployment was high, inflation was rampant, and anger and mistrust were spreading throughout Germany. This was his time to capture the nation, not by war but by constitutional means.

When Austria's biggest bank collapsed, it forced the banks in Berlin to close temporarily. Germany was unable to make its war payments, millions were unemployed as thousands of small businesses were wiped out. Deprived of jobs and ravaged by hunger, the Germans were willing to do anything to survive.

Hitler was delighted with the economic crisis; these were fertile times to gain the ear and vote of the masses. He campaigned against the Treaty of Versailles and assured Germans that if given a chance the country could become great again. Eventually, his time would come.

CONSTITUTIONAL ROOTS

"My parents voted for him because things were so bad, they believed they could not get any worse," a woman who survived the Nazi era told me. "They thought, why not give him a chance?" Millions of Germans agreed. And so it was that in July 1932 the Nazis emerged as the country's largest party, but they lacked a majority. A second election took place the same year, yet because of their ill-temper the Nazis fared worse at the polls, though they still represented the biggest single voting bloc. The pundits predicted that the Nazis had passed their prime.

Nevertheless, unemployment was high and the Communists were still a threat. Since there were numerous parties and none had a majority, the government found itself at a standstill. In desperation, Hindenburg appointed Hitler as chancellor on January 30, 1933. *He who now took the oath of office to uphold the Weimar Constitution would soon destroy it.*

Hitler knew, however, that according to the constitution his term of office depended on his ability to acquire majority support in the Reichstag. The Parliament could vote him out, or Hindenburg could dismiss him. He needed a majority he did not have. What he needed was a couple of miracles, and he got—or created—them.

Anticipating an election in March 1933 that he knew he could not win, Hitler apparently chose to create a crisis. On February 27, 1933, the Reichstag building in Berlin went up in flames. The evidence points to arson; most probably Hitler's men forced a Dutch man named Marinus van der Lubbe to enter the building through a passage used for the heating system. At gunpoint, he set a fire in the basement of the building, and soon the massive structure was in flames.

Hitler blamed the arson on a Communist conspiracy and induced Hindenburg to sign a decree "for the protection of the people and the state" that suspended individual liberties. The Nazis could then search homes without a warrant, confiscate property, and outlaw the meetings of groups that might oppose them. By signing the decree, Hindenburg was actually acting in accordance with the Weimar Constitution, which stipulated that the president could bypass Parliament in the event of an emergency. Little wonder Hitler said that the burning of the Reichstag was "a gift from the gods."

Though Hitler still failed to get a majority, by murder, threats, and promises, he did manage to get a two-thirds majority vote in the Reichstag to amend the constitution. By this amendment, all legislative functions were transferred to him personally. From then on, he, not the Reichstag, would make the laws. *On July 14, he decreed that the Nazis would be the sole political party in Germany.*

When conflict arose between the army and Hitler's rowdy "Brownshirts" (storm troopers), he made a deal with the army officers: If they would support him as Hindenburg's successor, he promised he would destroy the Treaty of Versailles and restore the army to its former strength. What is more, he would put an end to his Brownshirts who had roamed the streets and were now agitating for the right to replace the army.

When the generals agreed to his plan, he kept his word. He purged one thousand people on a single weekend (the weekend of "long knives"), many of them his own Brownshirts and other close friends who had helped put him in power. Hitler took full responsibility for the mass murders and told the Reichstag: "If anyone reproaches me and asks why I did not resort to the regular courts of justice, then all I can say is this: in this hour I was responsible for the fate of the German people. I became the Supreme Judge of the German people."[9]

The aged Hindenburg finally died, and before his body was scarcely cold Hitler held a ceremony in which all army officers swore an oath of personal loyalty to him and he proclaimed himself Führer and Reich chancellor.

The universal madness Nietzsche predicted had begun.

HISTORICAL REFLECTIONS

By and large the Germans offered little resistance to totalitarianism. I will talk more about the general apathy of the nation when we discuss Hitler's takeover of the church. For now read what Gerald Suster writes: "Many welcomed the abolition of individual responsibility for one's actions; for some it is easier to obey than to accept the dangers of freedom. Workers now had job security, a health service, cheap holiday schemes; if freedom meant starvation, then slavery was preferable."[10] *The man for whom the Germans had waited had arrived.*

As long as the economy was strong, people didn't care whether they had freedom of speech, freedom of travel, or freedom of elections. Under the Republic, people were starving in the big cities; bread on the table was more important than a ballot at a voting booth.

"It's the economy, stupid!" was the slogan of one nominee for American president in 1992. Though the claim was poor statesmanship, it was excellent politics. In Nazi Germany, as in every era, it was the economy that was the key to the political fortunes of a particular party or dictator. Even the Antichrist will count on the premise that most of us act as if our bodies are worth more than our souls.

HE WOULD TAKE THE CROSS OF CHRIST AND EXCHANGE IT FOR A BROKEN CROSS THAT HAD THE POWER TO MAKE GERMANY GREAT AGAIN.

One woman who lived in Germany during the Nazi era observed, "Hitler did more in a year than the Weimar Republic had done in ten." In a crisis it is easier for a strong leader to act quickly and decisively than to accomplish the nearly impossible task of building a consensus and threading legislation through a maze of committees. The Bible predicts that the time will come when the world will need a man who can act decisively and bypass the slow and unpredictable process of legislative gridlock.

If the economy is the key to physical survival and if the body is deemed more important than the soul, morality will soon be sacrificed in the interest of survival. The German people, at least initially, were willing to forgive Hitler's purges and his ruthless massacres in return for the right to live. Germans said simply that before Hitler they did have freedom—but with it came the freedom to starve.

With the existence of God wiped from the consciousness of the ruling elite and with the exaltation of the state above the laws of ordinary men, Hitler was free to pursue his goals. Dostoyevski was right: *If God does not exist everything is permissible.*

The man Rudolf Hess had described in his essay was then in place. A god had come into power, and millions would fall for his smooth seductions. He would take the cross of Christ with its emphasis on love and forgiveness and exchange it for a broken cross that had the power to make Germany great again. Hitler would not rest until his cross prevailed.

Now we turn to look at these events through the lens of Scripture. God was not simply watching from heaven. He is, after all, the One who raises up leaders and brings them down. We must see His fingerprints even in the course of Nazi history.

CHAPTER TWO

GOD AND HITLER: WHO WAS IN CHARGE?

"T oday it seems to me providential that Fate would have chosen Braunau on the Inn as my birthplace," wrote Adolf Hitler in the opening line of his famous book *Mein Kampf (My Struggle)*.[1] The man who is perhaps the most notorious dictator of all time repeatedly explained his role in the world as a responsibility given to him by "higher powers." His writings are filled with references to "Divine Providence" or what he simply calls Fate.

He believed that his birthplace was of special significance because it was located on the border of Germany and Austria. Though he does not say so, we also know that it was a hotbed of occult activity, and very probably young Adolf was introduced to powerful spiritual forces at an early age. More of that in the next chapter.

References to Providence or Fate are found in almost all of Hitler's speeches. After terrorizing the chancellor of Austria, Hitler marched into Vienna without firing a shot and then proclaimed to cheering crowds, "I believe that it was God's will to send a youth from here to the Reich, to raise him to be the leader of the nation so as to enable him to lead his homeland to the Reich. There is a higher ordering . . . I felt the call of Providence. And that which took place was only conceivable as the fulfillment of the wish and will of this Providence."[2] This providential "higher ordering" drove him.

He often thanked Providence for his successes. Speaking in Würzburg in 1937, he compared the individual with the larger force of Providence. The individual might be weak compared "with the omnipotence and will of Providence, yet at that moment when he acts as Providence would have him act he becomes immeasurably strong. Then there streams upon him that force. . . . And when I look back only on the five years which lie behind us, then I feel justified in saying: this has not been the work of man alone."[3] We should not be surprised that in *Mein Kampf* he wrote that he was doing "the will of the Lord."

Most interesting is his account of why he entered politics in the first place. Hitler was a messenger during World War I and was blinded by an attack of mustard gas. While he was recuperating in the hospital on Sunday, November 10, 1918, a pastor came to bring unbelievable news to the wounded soldiers in the military hospital: Germany had lost the war and a new government, a republic, had been proclaimed in Berlin! Hitler felt deep betrayal and experienced a conversion experience, a call to politics that he later described as "the pressure of destiny."

There in the hospital, with his eyes burning in darkness, he attained a spiritual vision that he later described as "the magical relationship between man and the whole Universe."[4] Fate "summoned" him to play a role in restoring the Fatherland.

The purpose of this chapter is to grapple with the question of how Hitler's understanding of Providence must be interpreted in light of the Bible's insistence that God rules in the affairs of men. We must answer the question, asked in different ways, as to what God was doing during the days of the Third Reich. Did God simply choose to abandon His responsibility as ruler of His world? Or was there a reason, perhaps not entirely clear to us, but a reason nonetheless for what happened?

God was doing many things in Nazi Germany, but I believe that the most important was the purification of His church. Just as Pharaoh was raised up by God that the power of the Almighty would be displayed, so Hitler was raised up so that God's power might again be made known. These terrible events judged the defiant Nazi leaders along with the apostate church leaders. They also refined the faith of the true believers who could give testimony of God's faithfulness even in distress.

Pastor Wilhelm Busch, an evangelist who survived the Nazi reign of terror, tells how he was arrested after holding evangelistic meetings in the city of Darmstadt. He was singled out of the crowd and pushed into a police car beside an official of the Gestapo. The SS man at the wheel was ordered to start driving. But the motor would not start. "Get going!" the officer shouted, as if the car would respond to his command. Just then from the midst of a crowd a young man standing on the steps of the church began to sing with a loud voice:

> Rejoice the Savior reigns
> The God of truth and love;
> When he had purged our stains,
> He took his seat above
> Lift up your heart, lift up your voice!
> Rejoice, again I say, rejoice!

The young man disappeared into the crowd, and the car started. Turning to the Gestapo officer, Pastor Busch said, "My poor friend! I am on the victor's side!"

The man was startled, then whispered, "A long time ago I used to be a member of the YMCA."

"Well!" the pastor replied. "And now you are arresting Christians! Poor man, I wouldn't want to be in your shoes." In a few moments they reached the prison, but the triumph of Christ had opened before the evangelist.[5] The renewed conviction of God's sovereignty had encouraged him at the hour of need. Those who saw only meaningless suffering in Nazi Germany were carried along by the Nazi tidal wave; those who saw God had the strength to withstand it.

> Two men sit in prison bars;
> One sees mud, the other stars.

Yes, the Savior was reigning even in Nazi Germany! The biblical doctrine of Divine Providence gave Christians such as Pastor Busch the confidence to believe that the suffering of the German church was not in vain. If we understand God's Providence correctly, we will be convinced that, for God's people, no suffering is ever meaningless. Those who could see the overruling hand of God, even in Nazism, had the courage to withstand the persecution. They were convinced that God never fails His people, even when they are asked to pay the supreme price for their faith.

What does it mean to say that God reigned in Germany, when it seems so obvious that Hitler was in charge? And to what should we attribute those remarkable acts of Providence by which Hitler was allowed to terrorize the world?

Join me on a tour that begins with a series of incidents that confirm Hitler's preoccupation with the doctrine of Fate, or Providence, and ends with the conviction that God rules "all things by the counsel of His own will." We will try to sort out the Third Reich from a biblical perspective. In the end we will see why God can be trusted even if we should someday be asked to walk through a similar forbidding valley.

You may be as surprised as I at the twists and turns of Providence, or "higher ordering," in Hitler's life. He had every reason to believe that he had been destined to greatness; higher powers decreed that he would play a special role in the world, and all the cards appeared stacked in his favor.

THE MIRACLES OF PROVIDENCE

On numerous occasions Hitler should have been killed; at other times he was so thoroughly disgraced that he should have been banished rather than worshiped as "the Führer." Scan his life and you will be amazed at the number of times that only Providence can account for his remarkable career.

HIS BIRTH

Hitler was born in Braunau, Austria, at 6:30 in the evening on April 20, 1889. What an unlikely birthplace for a peasant who would eventually win the worship of millions of otherwise restrained and sober-minded Germans! Even here it was a twist of fate that decreed that he would survive infancy and live to have a short, memorable name.

By all accounts, Adolf Hitler should have been named Adolf Schicklgruber. His father, Alois, was an illegitimate son who took the name of his mother, Maria Schicklgruber. Maria eventually married a wandering miller who disappeared for years at a time. The man did not legitimatize his wife's son, so Alois, who would become Hitler's father, kept his mother's maiden name for thirty-nine years.

Incredibly, this wandering husband showed up at age eighty-four and decided to accept the paternity of his wife's illegitimate son (many believe that he may have been the father of Alois in the first place). At any rate, in his old age the stepfather accepted his wife's thirty-nine-year-old son as his own and gave him a new name—Alois Schicklgruber became Alois Hitler. If this old man had not appeared out of nowhere, the name change would not have happened.

William Shirer, in his monumental work *The Rise and Fall of the Third Reich,* says it is difficult to imagine Germans using the comical greeting, "Heil Schicklgruber!"[6] The chant "Heil Hitler!" was not only memorable but militaristic and in keeping with the pageantry of the massive Nazi rallies. Even Hitler himself looked back upon his father's change of name as one more indication of "favorable Providence."

As for Hitler's father, Alois, he took up with many women during his careers—first as a shoemaker, then as a customs official. His third wife was Klara Poelzl, who would become the mother of Adolf Hitler. Because Alois and Klara were second cousins, they found it necessary to receive a special dispensation to be married.

So it was that Hitler was the third child of his father's third marriage. Klara's first two children died in infancy; Adolf was, of course, spared by Fate, or Providence; the fourth child died at the age of six. Only the fifth child, Paula, lived to survive her infamous brother.

HE VOLUNTEERED FOR RISKY ASSIGNMENTS, NOT SO MUCH BECAUSE OF HIS BRAVERY BUT BECAUSE HE BELIEVED FATE HAD DECREED THAT HE WAS INVINCIBLE.

Think of how different the history of the world would have been if Adolf had died in infancy as did two of his brothers and a sister. If any one of the other children had survived in his stead, humanly speaking, Germany would have been spared the stunning heights of grandeur and the future devastation brought to much of Europe and the world. As far as we know, the Holocaust would not have happened.

Can anyone deny that it was God who, at least indirectly, determined that Hitler would have a name that sounded pleasant to the German people and that he would survive his childhood?

Hitler was confident that he was being guided by a higher hand.

WORLD WAR I

When World War I began, Hitler welcomed the opportunity to end his days of hunger (by now he had moved from Vienna to Munich) and joined the German army. As an Austrian, he had to apply for special permission to volunteer for military service. In his first battle against the British at Ypres, only 600 of the 3,500 men in his regiment survived. He spent most of the war at the front and lived through some of the fiercest conflicts. Though shells exploded and killed others, his life was always spared.

As a messenger, he volunteered for difficult assignments, believing he had an uncanny ability to avert disaster. While eating in a bunker, he suddenly rose from the table and went elsewhere to finish his meal. Moments later a bomb landed where he had been seated, killing his comrades.

He volunteered for risky assignments, not so much because of his bravery but because he believed Fate had decreed that he was invincible. By running through a hail of bullets, he was "tempting Providence," assuring himself that he could not die until his mission was fulfilled. Twice he was decorated for bravery. In four years of combat, he suffered only a leg injury and the temporary blindness referred to earlier.

Little wonder that in his personal letters he affirmed that he owed his life to a miracle, or rather to a whole series of miracles. He believed he was called to the role that higher powers had chosen for him.

THE PUTSCH

The Communist revolution in Russia occurred in 1918—the same year Germany surrendered, ending World War I. The Communist party in Germany was growing in strength, positioning itself for a takeover. The soldiers who returned from the war were angry men who could not find jobs; Hitler later described them as men who favored revolution for its own sake and "desired to see revolution established as a permanent condition." We have already seen that the democratic government organized in Weimar was despised.

When Hitler returned to his adopted city of Munich, he was assigned a job in the press and news bureau of the political department of the army's district command. He was asked to attend a meeting of a small socialist party, but he left unimpressed. He decided not to return; but when an invitation arrived, he reconsidered.

After some misgivings, he enrolled as the seventh member of the committee of the German Workers' Party. Later, under his control, they added the words "National Socialist"; hence the National Socialist German Workers' Party was born (later dubbed the *Nazis*). Hitler maneuvered to get control of the leadership and used it to build his political base.

In 1923, when Germany was rampant with political chaos and runaway inflation, Hitler believed the time was ripe for a Putsch (revolution) that would enable him to take over Germany. On November 8 of that year, he seized control of a meeting of three thousand men gathered in the *Bürgerbräukeller* (beer hall) in Munich by shooting his pistol into the air, ascending the podium, and proclaiming that his revolution had begun! Everyone had to get on board or be confronted by six hundred of his men who had surrounded the building. He went to the podium shouting that the Bavarian government had been removed and that the army and police were now marching under the banner of the swastika. He was bluffing, of course, but the people didn't know it.

Hitler took the three politicians who were leading the meeting into a nearby room and ordered them at gunpoint to unite with his party. When they refused, he ran back into the hall and announced that a new government had just been formed with the respected Ludendorff (the defeated but popular military general of World War I) at the head of the army. Loud cheers rose in the beer hall while the three leaders were still locked up in the small room next to the podium.

An aide had been summoned to bring General Ludendorff to the meeting. When the general arrived and heard that Hitler had pulled his surprise, he was angry. He was even angrier when he heard that Hitler and not Ludendorff was to be the head of the new government. Yet, forced by the political events of the day and the pressure of the moment, the general convinced the three leaders to join in the revolution. Moments later they went back to the podium and announced to the awestruck crowd that they had pledged support to the new regime!

Thanks to poor planning, the "new government" unraveled overnight. The three men who pledged their allegiance at gunpoint turned against Hitler. To save face, the next day Hitler agreed to a plan suggested by General Ludendorff that the "Brownshirts" march to the center of Munich to take it over. Together the two men led a column of three thousand storm troopers to the center of the city. A flag bearing the swastika was unfurled at the head of the column with men and weapons following. Crowds accompanied them.

As they marched through the narrow *Residenzstrasse* (Residents Street), which opens up to the spacious Odeonsplatz, they met a contingent of police officers. No one knows who fired first, but a volley of shots rang out from both sides, and in sixty seconds sixteen Nazis and three police officers had been hit. Hitler had been walking with his left arm locked in the right arm of a comrade; his comrade was shot and fell, pulling Hitler down to the pavement. Witnesses said Hitler was the first to get up and turn back, leaving his comrades dead or dying on the street.

Hitler was whisked by limousine to the countryside home of a friend to recuperate, complaining that he had dislocated his arm. He had been thoroughly discredited and knew it. Newspapers around the world proclaimed that his career was over. Little wonder he contemplated suicide, sitting for hours at a time with a gun pointed to his head. He was talked out of the deed by his friend's wife and daughter who nursed him back to health. Again we can only speculate how the history of Germany would read if he had had the courage to pull the trigger.

Even Hitler's friends were embarrassed at the stupidity of trying to overthrow the Bavarian government. Even if they had been successful, they could never have captured the rest of Germany. But Hitler, as we are learning, always seemed to defy the odds.

Two days later Hitler was arrested and tried for treason. As Fate would have it, his twenty-four-day trial made him famous, capturing headlines around the world. He was given an unlimited opportunity to make speeches, and he used colorful oratory to get his message to all of Germany and, for that matter, to the world. He was convicted of treason and spent ten months in the Landsberg Prison where he and Rudolf Hess wrote the Nazi bible, *Mein Kampf.*

How did he view those events years later? He saw in them the hand of Providence. He believed that if his Putsch had succeeded in Munich it would have been the end of him, for at the time he did not have the power to sustain a revolution throughout Germany. His failure was for his good.

Listen to his interpretation of his initial failure:

> We knew that we were carrying out the will of Providence, and we were being guided by a higher power. . . . Fate meant well with us. It did not permit an action to succeed which, if it had succeeded, would in the end have inevitably crashed as a result of the movement's inner immaturity in those days and its deficient organizational and intellectual foundation.[7]

Fate caused him to fail on one day so that he might succeed at another time. Later, he was given the chancellorship just when support for the Nazi party was in decline. That he should have been able to manipulate, convince, and threaten the Reichstag to give him dictatorial powers —the twists and turns of Fate are remarkable indeed. No wonder he accepted the worship of the German people. He believed there was no obstacle in his career that Fate could not overcome.

THE ASSASSINATION ATTEMPTS

By 1944 Fate had protected Hitler from at least a half-dozen assassination attempts. One of these miscarried when a time bomb planted in his airplane failed to explode; when the mechanism was later checked, no reason could be found why the bomb did not detonate.

Bitterly disappointed, the conspirators decided that the next time they had to succeed. Colonel Gersdorff agreed to a suicide mission. He would conceal two bombs in his overcoat, set the fuses, and stay as close to Hitler as possible during ceremonies in Berlin. He would blow himself up along with the Führer and his entourage.

The plan was to let Hitler give his speech, then Gersdorff would set the fuses and stay with Hitler for the fifteen minutes needed for the weapons to explode. But as Fate would have it, it was announced that Hitler would be staying only five minutes after the speech rather

German troops entered the Sudetenland in Czechoslovakia on October 1, 1938. Two days later Hitler makes his triumphal entry.

than the planned half hour. Obviously, the fuses were never set. The change in plans spared his life.

The most famous assassination attempt was carried out by Stauffenberg, a respected army officer. Though initially a reluctant supporter of Hitler, he soon joined a growing cadre of conspirators who hoped to kill the demonic leader.

When I visited the old military headquarters in Berlin, which now contains a museum to the Resistance movement, I was surprised at how detailed the plans were to set up a new government. They had already decided who would be in charge of the various departments, the cabinet, and the negotiations with the West. The plans called for complete control of Berlin within two hours after the death of the dictator. All that was necessary was that Hitler be assassinated.

To the conspirators' delight, Stauffenberg was promoted to full colonel, which meant that he now had direct access to Hitler. After several failed attempts due to canceled meetings or unexpected happenstance, his opportunity finally came.

Colonel Stauffenberg flew to meet with Hitler and his generals at Rastenburg. He was allowed to pass through heavy security, and shortly after noon he excused himself to go into the rest room where he prepared the bomb. He broke a capsule of acid that would eat through the wire; that would loose the strike hammer and cause the bomb to detonate.

When he entered the meeting room, Hitler was seated at the center of the long side of the table, his back to the door, with his staff standing around him, poring over maps. The Führer paused to greet Stauffenberg and told him he would hear his report shortly. Stauffenberg took his place at the table a few feet to the right of Hitler. He put his briefcase on the floor, shoving it under the table about six feet from Hitler's legs. There were five minutes to go.

Stauffenberg excused himself, saying he needed to make an urgent phone call. Colonel Brandt, absorbed in what was being said, leaned over the table to see the map. Since Stauffenberg's briefcase was in the way, he reached down with one hand and lifted it to the far side of the table. This gesture saved Hitler's life and cost Brandt his.

At precisely 12:42 P.M. on July 20, 1944, the bomb went off. Stauffenberg, who was watching from several hundred yards away, saw bodies fly out of windows and debris hurled everywhere. There was not a doubt in his mind that everyone in the room was either dead or dying.

A telegram with the news that the assassination was a success can be seen in the museum to the Resistance in Berlin. Stauffenberg was able to make his way through the checkpoints and fly back to Berlin, confident that he had been successful. After he landed, he discovered that the conspirators had done nothing to consolidate their power. He also discovered, much to his dismay, that Hitler had not been killed. Colonel Brandt's act of shoving the briefcase to the far side of the room under the sturdy oak table had saved Hitler's life.

Four men were killed, but Hitler was only shaken—he had some burns, his right arm had been bruised, and his eardrums were punctured. But soon he was in charge of his senses. He even kept his appointment with Mussolini at four o'clock that afternoon.

To what did Hitler attribute this miraculous preservation of his life? Not to luck, but to Fate. To Mussolini he said, "It is obvious that nothing is going to happen to me; undoubtedly it is my Fate to continue on my way and bring my task to completion. . . . Having now escaped death . . . I am more than ever convinced that the great cause which I serve will be brought through its present perils and that everything will be brought to a good end."[8]

Within hours of the blast, Stauffenberg was fingered as the perpetrator of the act. He was executed late that evening, and within a few weeks thousands of others who were suspected as being part of the conspiracy were brutally murdered. By one o'clock the next morning, Hitler broadcast an address to the nation, assuring them that he was fine and that he would punish those who were responsible for this despicable act. He had been spared because he had a job to do. He said, "I regard this as a confirmation of the task imposed upon me by Providence."[9] He told his valet that this was new proof that he had been selected by Providence to lead Germany to victory.

As late as January of 1945, he told his soldiers, "I bear this my lot to Providence which has considered me worthy enough to take on . . . this decisive work in the history of the German people."[10] In his last days, he complained bitterly that "Fate had denied him the victory" he wanted. Thus on April 30, 1945, he committed suicide in his bunker in Berlin. The Fate to which he attributed his greatness was also the Fate by which he died. The invisible hand that raised him up also brought him down.

IS GOD ONLY INVOLVED WHEN RIGHTEOUS LEADERS ARE INSTALLED AND UNINVOLVED WHEN A LEADER IS SOMETHING LESS THAN DISTINCTIVELY CHRISTIAN, OR EVEN EVIL?

What do we make of Hitler's overwhelming conviction that he was ruling by the will of Fate? Who was in charge? What role does God play in the affairs of men? What role does Satan play? And what about Hitler himself—what was his role?

AN INTERPRETATION OF PROVIDENCE

The Bible is filled with references to what theologians call the Providence of God, the fact that the Almighty has not left the world to run by itself but is actively involved in the affairs of men. Berkhof captured the biblical teaching. Providence "is that continual exercise of the divine energy whereby the Creator preserves all His creatures, is operative in all that comes to pass in the world, and directs all things to their appointed end."[11]

Here are five pillars on which we can build a doctrine of divine Providence. Let me encourage you to read this chapter to the end before you draw any conclusions. We have to navigate some deep theological waters, and I want to make sure that we arrive at our destination together!

1. GOD RULES IN THE AFFAIRS OF MEN

When Mr. Clinton was elected president in 1992, I heard a Christian preacher say, "God had nothing to do with the election of this president; the people made the choice!"

I found that statement incredible for several reasons. First, I wonder what that teacher would have said if a president had been elected who was distinctively Christian and consciously committed to ruling with biblical principles. Would he have said that that president had been raised up by God for this hour of American history? To put it differently: Is God only involved when righteous leaders are installed and uninvolved when a leader is something less than distinctively Christian, or even evil?

Second, I wonder how this teacher would interpret the dozens of Scriptures that pointedly say that it is God who sets up rulers and brings them down? We cannot deny, and should not want to deny, that God is actively supervising and directing the political structure of the world. Daniel says that God changes the times and the epochs, and "He removes kings and establishes kings" (2:21). Lest we think we have misunderstood, he repeats it even more clearly: "In order that the living may know that the Most High is ruler over the realm of mankind, and bestows it on whom He wishes, and sets over it the lowliest of men" (4:17).

"The Lord of Hosts" is a phrase that occurs hundreds of times in the Old Testament to affirm that behind the visible rulers of the world is the invisible God of the universe.

Little wonder that God can speak of the pagan king Cyrus as His servant (Isaiah 45:1) and can say to the prophet Habakkuk, "For behold, I am raising up the Chaldeans, that fierce and impetuous people who march throughout the earth to seize dwelling places which are not theirs" (1:6). The New Testament reinforces this conclusion. Remember when Pilate was exasperated with Christ who refused to answer him? He said to Christ with an air of defiance, "Do You not know that I have authority to release You, and I have authority to crucify You?" Christ calmly put it all in theological perspective, "You would have no authority over Me, unless it had been given you from above; for this reason he who delivered Me up to you has the greater sin" (John 19:10–11).

HITLER WAS A THOROUGHLY DEMONIZED BEING WHOSE BODY WAS BUT THE SHELL FOR THE SPIRIT THAT INHABITED HIM.

Paul, when writing to the church at Rome during the days of Nero, stated clearly, "For there is no authority except from God, and those which exist are established by God" (Romans 13:1). God did not abandon His role in world affairs in pagan Rome or in pagan Germany.

Certainly Hitler could not have ruled except that it was "given to him by God." He would have had no power at all, unless it were granted from above. God rules!

2. GOD DELEGATES HIS AUTHORITY TO ANGELS, SATAN, AND PEOPLE

How shall we interpret Hitler's constant references to Fate or Providence? It is rather obvious that the voices he heard and the powers from which he drew his strength were not from God but from Satan. As we shall learn in the next chapter, Hitler was a thoroughly demonized being whose body was but the shell for the spirit that inhabited him. When he predicted that the Third Reich would last a thousand years, it was a typical instance of how Satan often overreaches; he cannot predict the future with accuracy because he cannot control it. Perhaps no man in history was so clearly indwelt by dark, cruel demons.

In what sense then can we say that it was God who raised Hitler up and took him down? *Hitler was held, figuratively speaking, in Satan's hands; but Satan, for all of his evil, is always held in God's hands.* Luther reminded us that even the Devil is God's devil.

The Almighty created the world; He created Lucifer, who sinned and became Satan; He is the one who supervises and directs everything that comes to pass through secondary causes. Nothing happens but that God has agreed to let it happen and has established those conditions that make events possible. Thus God remained the ruler among men even when Hitler, under the power of Satan, was in control.

God sets the parameters by which Satan must abide. It is God who says, "So much and no more." Satan and men have only the latitude the Almighty prescribes. From a human perspective, Hitler alone was ruling in Nazi Germany. But he could not have ruled without God's consent and supervision. As Paul reminds us, God "works all things after the counsel of His will" (Ephesians 1:11). Some prefer to call it His "permissive will," but it is His will nevertheless. He directs all things to their appointed end.

Regardless of your theological viewpoint, you will have to agree that the Holocaust would not have happened if God had not chosen to permit it. Figuratively speaking, He initialed the memo; He gave the green light. Since He chose to permit it, He could also have chosen to not permit it. That's why the Bible can say that there is no power except for God and that God rules in the affairs of men. He did not *do* the evil, but He chose to let evil happen.

Here's where it gets tricky. Even though evil is contrary to God's nature—and contrary to His revealed Word—God permits it nevertheless. Obviously, the Almighty does that to achieve an ultimate objective. God is willing to override some of His own desires to accomplish a greater purpose. God permits and approves all that ever comes to pass. He even permits what He hates.

If you are unconvinced, remember that someday another will arise who will revive Hitler's agenda. He will be worshiped not merely by one country but by the world. He will perform economic and spiritual wonders. He will persecute Israel, trying desperately to wipe out the Jewish state. He, like Hitler, will believe that he is raised up by Fate. His meteoric career will be ascribed to the fact that he will have been "summoned by higher powers."

The Antichrist is called "the beast" in Revelation 13. We read, "And the dragon gave him his power and his throne and great authority. . . . and they worshiped the dragon, because he gave his authority to the beast" (Revelation 13:2, 4). Four times in a few verses we read that his power was "given to him."

Although many of us believe we will be raptured to be with Christ before Antichrist takes control, the extent of his authority should make us shudder in amazement. "And it was given to him to make war with the saints and to overcome them; and authority over every tribe and people and tongue and nation was given to him. And all who dwell on the earth will worship him, everyone whose name has not been written from the foundation of the world in the book of life of the Lamb who has been slain" (vv. 7–8).

Antichrist's authority is given to him by Satan, but Satan's authority is given to him by God.

The reason God can predict that Antichrist's authority will last only forty-two months is because this evil man's influence depends on God's will. What has been "given to him" will also be taken away. He could not rule unless it had "been given him from heaven" (John 3:27).

God hates the idolatry of the Antichrist, just as He hated the idolatry of the German people. But God permits it nevertheless. Obviously He is directing the events of the world to an appointed end; He uses wars and persecution as a judgment against unbelievers and as chastisement of the church. In the end His purposes will be accomplished and His name glorified.

Those Christians in Nazi Germany who believed that evil was triumphing because God was too weak to stem the tide could find no hope in their distress. But believers who knew that God still ruled even when Hitler was in power could be assured that they would be compensated for any sacrifice they would make. They were sustained by this biblical conviction:

> Therefore we do not lose heart, but though our outer man is decaying, yet our inner man is being renewed day by day. For momentary, light affliction is producing for us an eternal weight of glory far beyond all comparison, while we look not at the things which are seen, but at the things which are not seen; for the things which are seen are temporal, but the things which are not seen are eternal. (2 Corinthians 4:16–18)

As Paul says elsewhere, "For I consider that the sufferings of this present time are not worthy to be compared with the glory that is to be revealed to us" (Romans 8:18).

All authority is delegated by God. This gives us confidence even when wicked rulers rise to power. Persecution always divides the sheep from the goats; it either drives people into the arms of God or abandons them to their just fate. God was doing more in Nazi Germany than we will ever realize.

3. GOD HOLDS ANGELS, SATAN, AND PEOPLE RESPONSIBLE FOR THE EVIL THAT HE LETS THEM DO

Here we seem to reach an impasse. Since God has ultimate control, is He an accomplice in men's evil deeds? That was the dilemma that evidently caused Einstein to reject belief in a personal God. He argued that if God were truly all-powerful, then every human thought and action is also His work. Therefore in giving out punishment and rewards, Einstein said, "He would to a certain extent be passing judgment on Himself. How can this be combined with the goodness and righteousness ascribed to Him?"[12]

Einstein was expressing what most of us have struggled with. How can God hold human beings responsible if they are simply fulfilling His will? A complete discussion of this question is well beyond the scope of this chapter, but in general we can say that the personal beings God created have enough independence to make them accountable for their deeds.

Notice carefully that the title of this chapter is not: "God *or* Hitler: Who Was in Charge?"; but rather it is "God *and* Hitler." God had His part—He was doing the *delegating*. Hitler and Satan were doing their part—they were doing the *destroying*.

God is in charge because He is the Creator and sets the limits; Hitler was responsible because of what he chose to do within those divine parameters. God did not do evil when He delegated authority to Hitler; however, Hitler did evil by misusing that authority. What is more, God does not pass judgment on Himself because there is no standard outside of Himself to which He must conform.

So if we consider the larger picture, Hitler (though controlled by Satan) ruled according to the permission and discretion of God Almighty. God gave Satan the latitude to deceive Hitler; and Hitler himself made choices that led him into such deceptions.

4. HISTORY WILL END ACCORDING TO GOD'S PLAN

There should be no doubt in our minds that history will end as God predicted. Speaking of believers Paul wrote that we have "been predestined according to His purpose who works all things after the counsel of His will" (Ephesians 1:11). Obviously rebellion against God is futile. Regardless who appears to be winning today, God wins in the end.

While watching movie clips from Hitler's Germany, I couldn't help but think how different it all would have been if the Christians had remembered that eternity is more important than time! It's a lesson we need to remember even before persecution comes our way.

5. WE CAN REST ON THE WISDOM OF GOD'S WAYS

This doctrine of Providence with all of its mystery is nevertheless a pillow on which we can rest our weary souls.

Hitler used the terms *Fate* and *Providence* interchangeably. But in light of his career, he would have been more precise if he had used the term *Fate* exclusively. For he had entrusted himself to Satan, who could make great promises but in the end could not deliver. And Hitler, his pawn, passed those false promises on to the German people.

The word *Fate* is best used to describe a power that is finite, a power that has no guaranteed outcome, a power whose plans and aspirations might well be thwarted. The Fate about which Hitler spoke could not know the end results of World War II; that Fate made Hitler a victim of forces beyond his control. That Fate could control only those events that were granted by a higher Providence.

Strictly speaking, only Christians can rest in the doctrine of Providence; that is, the fact that the world is governed by a God who is capable of working all things toward an appointed end. It is this Providence that sees the sparrow fall to the ground and knows the number of hairs on our heads.

Christians do not believe in Fate with its blind alleys and dashed hopes. Those who have come to know Christ are convinced that they are in the hands of a God who knows the end from the beginning and works all things together for good.

We live not by *Fate* but by *faith*. Fate leads to doom; faith leads to destiny. "That the proof of your faith, being more precious than gold which is perishable, even though tested by fire, may be found to result in praise and glory and honor at the revelation of Jesus Christ" (1 Peter 1:7).

YOUR RESPONSE TO DIVINE PROVIDENCE

There are three possible responses to God's providence.

First, there is *atheism*. We have met those who tell us that no God could see the atrocities of this world (e.g., the Holocaust) and not intervene. We must be sensitive to such a reaction because it is difficult to understand how a good God could permit (and hence ordain) such evil. But atheism is very unsatisfying; it affirms not only that we have horrific injustice in the world, but also that justice will never triumph.

I have a Jewish friend who does not believe in a personal God precisely because of the Holocaust. But he seemed perturbed when I reminded him one day that according to his view, Hitler and his henchmen would never be judged for what they did. In an atheistic world not only is this world unjust, but there can be no justice. Atheism teaches that our cry for justice will never be satisfied.

The second response is *anger*—vindictive anger against God. Some people are so bitter toward God because of the terrors of this world that they shut Him out of their lives. One angry person said to me, "If there is a God, he must be the devil!"

Again, let us be honest enough to admit that we have all wrestled with such thoughts. We ask, Why did Hitler not die in infancy with his brothers and sister? Why did he walk out of the mess hall and miss being killed by a bomb? Why did the assassination attempts fail? Why did God initial the memo that in effect said, "You are permitted to do the evil you have planned"?

Such anger is understandable but destructive. Anger toward God is futile, wasted energy. No one who vents his or her anger at God wins. We may not like what He does, but since He doesn't ask us how to run His universe, we hurt only ourselves. You can't sink a battleship with a peashooter.

Worse, those who are angry with God miss being comforted by His attributes of love, mercy, and forgiveness. It is better to admit simply that we cannot fathom the mystery of God's ways than to turn away from the only One who can help us. Since He knows more than we do, since He sees eternity and we don't, it is best to believe that we would agree with Him if we had all the facts.

A third option in the presence of the God who rules our cruel world is *awe*. In light of the fact that God is so terrifying, because He has permitted all kinds of atrocities to take place in His universe, we should be motivated to prepare to meet Him one-on-one after death. No wonder we read that it is a "fearful thing to fall into the hands of the living God."

Liberal theologians have promoted foolish theories teaching that the God of the Old Testament was a cruel God, whereas the God of the New is loving and kind and would never send anyone to hell. We can answer them by saying, "Just look at the Holocaust!" You don't need to believe the Bible to see that there is a side to God other than unrestrained love.

Because of the terror He has allowed on this planet, because His ways are beyond our comprehension, because He is holy, we should take advantage of the gift of His Son to our planet. Only Christ can shield us from the wrath of God that will come to all sinners after death. "He who believes in the Son has eternal life; but he who does not obey the Son shall not see life, but the wrath of God abides on him" (John 3:36).

THE STORY OF NAZI GERMANY IS REALLY THE STORY OF CONFLICT BETWEEN TWO SAVIORS AND TWO CROSSES.

The rebellious can take no comfort in the fact that nothing happens in the world without divine permission. But to the ones who can call God their Father, it is of great comfort to know that all things that come our way do so because of God's providential leading. Not only the great events of history, but even the most minute occurrences are subject to God's direction. And He knows how to turn evil to good.

John Calvin's words would have given comfort to the Christians who withstood the Nazi regime. "Let them recall that the devil and the whole cohort of the wicked are completely restrained by God's hand as by a bridle, so that they are unable either to hatch any plot against us or, having hatched it, to make preparations or, if they have fully planned it, to stir a finger towards carrying it out, except so far as he had permitted, indeed commanded them." The atrocities of Nazism only gave unbelievers more reasons to disbelieve; the faith of believers who clung to God's promises was sustained.

Whether in the Third Reich or the Last Reich, the God of the universe rules. Blessed are those who submit themselves directly into His hands rather than into the hands of those fallible creatures to whom He has delegated authority.

The story of Nazi Germany is really the story of conflict between two saviors and two crosses. Eventually the church was forced to choose, because in the end only one cross could triumph.

Keep reading.

CHAPTER THREE

THE RELIGION OF THE THIRD REICH: THEN AND NOW

T he prediction was both astonishing and accurate.

In 1834, one hundred years before Hitler, a poet named Heinrich Heine assessed the mood in Germany and concluded that only the cross of Christ was holding back the Germans' "lust for war." The prediction was even more remarkable because Heine was a Jew, a man who nevertheless believed that only Christianity could tame what he called that "brutal German joy in battle."

Heine, who possibly did not understand why the Cross had supernatural power, called it a *talisman,* an object with magical power that held aggression at bay in the German nation. And should the Cross be broken, the forces of brutality would break out and the world would be filled with "terror and astonishment."

Read the rest of his assessment, which turned out to be more accurate than he could have ever known:

> Should the subduing talisman, the Cross, break, then will come roaring forth the wild madness of the old champions, the insane Berserker rage [the rage of the ferocious Norse warriors] of which the Northern poets sing. That talisman is brittle, and the day will come when it will pitifully

break. The old stone Gods will rise from the long-forgotten ruin and rub the dust of a thousand years from their eyes; and Thor, leaping to life with his giant hammer, will crush the Gothic cathedrals.[1]

That prediction, of course, was fulfilled with the coming of Hitler. The cross of Christ was broken, formed into a *hakenkreuz* (broken cross) that became a symbol of the Nazi agenda. When this pagan cross replaced the cross of the crucified Redeemer, the pagan gods came out of hiding and the world trembled. Thor, the ancient Nordic god of thunder and war, took up his hammer, and the cathedrals of Germany were crushed both literally and symbolically. If the church in America should accept a counterfeit cross, we just might fare no better.

Hitler admired Guido von List, who as a boy in Vienna vowed before an altar in St. Stefan's Cathedral that when he became an adult he would build a temple to the ancient German god Wotan. List used the swastika for his occult religion, believing that it was a link to an ancient race of Germanic priests. It was also a symbol found in Hindu and Buddhist relics. He founded a secret blood brotherhood called Armanen, which had substituted the swastika for the Cross in rituals involving sexual perversion and the practice of medieval magic.

His members used the *Heil!* (Hail!) greeting that would later become the hallmark of Nazi worship. List was a rabid anti-Semite who railed against the Jews and worshiped the glories of the pure blood of the Aryan (German) race. Before he died in 1919, he predicted that there would be a racially pure community in Germany that would destroy democracy and Jewry.[2]

In his early days in Vienna, Hitler met List and knew of his secret society that promised to "unlock the secrets of the universe." And when Hitler's Nazis were mobilized, he borrowed the swastika as its symbol, trying out several designs and finally choosing one that was to his liking. The three colors (red, white, and black), he said, "form the most brilliant harmony in existence."

"A Symbol it really is!" he exclaimed in *Mein Kampf*. "In *red* we see the social idea of the movement; in *white* the nationalistic idea, in the *swastika* the mission of the struggle for the victory of the Aryan man."[3] Though the cross of Christ was later embedded within the swastikas that adorned German churches, Hitler was not satisfied. *His*

stated plan was to have the swastika replace the cross of Christ altogether. A new messiah called for a new cross.

The meaning of this new cross cannot be understood apart from Hitler's "call" to messiahship. The new cross symbolized a new religion.

THE NEW MESSIAH

"Follow Hitler! He will dance but it is I who have called the tune! I have initiated him into the 'Secret Doctrine,' opened his centres in vision and given him the means to communicate with the Powers. Do not mourn for me: I shall have influenced history more than any other German."[4]

So spoke Dietrich Eckart as he lay dying in 1923. Eckart was one of the seven founders of the Nazi party and a dedicated satanist, a man immersed in black magic and the Thule group of occultists. Eckart had been looking for a pupil, someone whom he could introduce to the spiritual forces, someone to catapult Germany to the dizzying heights of world conquest. In a series of séances, he claims that he had a "satanic annunciation" that he was destined to prepare the vessel for the Antichrist, the man who would inspire the world and lead the Aryan race to world conquest. When he met Hitler he said, "Here is the one for whom I was but the prophet and forerunner."[5]

After Eckart's death, Karl Haushofer became Hitler's spiritual mentor, taking him through the deepest levels of occult transformation until he became a thoroughly demonized being. Hitler was even transformed sexually; he became a sadomasochist, practicing various forms of sexual perversion. He was stimulated sexually by violence, brutality, and blood. Hermann Rauschning, a friend of Hitler who later defected to the Allies, said of him, "Hatred is like wine to him, it intoxicates him . . . he had the instincts of a sadist finding sexual excitement in torturing others."[6]

Haushofer had made several trips to India and was well versed in Eastern occultism. He also lived in Japan for a time where he was initiated into an esoteric Buddhist society called the Green Dragon. Through these contacts a colony of Tibetan lamas settled in Berlin, and when the Russians took the city in 1945, they found a thousand Tibetan corpses in German uniforms. Haushofer, more than any other, challenged Hitler with the vision of world conquest.

Thus a new religion with a new cross was begun; an ancient broken cross was used to rally the masses. Hitler stated openly that it was his intention to begin a new religion, a religion that would accomplish what Christianity had failed to bring about. Christianity, by honoring mercy and forgiveness, had weakened the German nation. In contrast, Hitler's religion would be "a joyous message that liberated men from the things that burdened their life. We should no longer have any fear of death and a bad conscience." This new religion would restore the greatness of Germany, avenge the failures of the past, and map out the blueprint for a grand future. Men "would be able to trust their instincts, would no longer be citizens of two worlds, but would be rooted in the single eternal life of this world."[7]

Hitler offered himself as a messiah with a divine mission to save Germany. On one occasion he displayed the whip he often carried to demonstrate that "in driving out the Jews I remind myself of Jesus in the temple." He declared, "Just like Christ, I have a duty to my own people." He even boasted that just as Christ's birth had changed the calendar so his victory over the Jews would be the beginning of a new age. "What Christ began," he said, "I will complete." In a speech just days after becoming chancellor, he parodied the Lord's Prayer, promising that under him a new kingdom would come on earth and that his would be "the power and the glory. Amen." He added that if he did not fulfill his mission, "you should then crucify me."[8]

Hitler made other claims reminiscent of Christ. If Christ had His "elect," Hitler had his too. He promised, "Whoever proclaims his allegiance to me is by this very proclamation and the manner in which it is made, one of the chosen." Just as Jesus suffered at the hands of Jews, so the Nazis believed they also were suffering, crucified by the betrayal of the Jews in World War I; now a new Germany was resurrected with vigor and hope.

We have learned that Hitler had a vision, a mystical "call" into politics that launched his remarkable career. The date was important to him because he was just under thirty years old, the same age as another Messiah who came to save mankind. In July of 1937, he remarked, "God has created this people and it has grown according to his will. And it is according to our will [nach unserem Willen] it shall remain and never pass away." He fancied himself not just the leader of the Christian world but of the non-Christian world he planned to conquer. "I'm going to become a religious figure. Soon I'll be the great

Hitler preaching to his earliest supporters in the Sterneckerbrau about 1920.
A painting entitled "In the beginning was the Word," by Herman Otto Hoyer.

chief of the Tartars. Already Arabs and Moroccans are mingling my name with their prayers."[9]

Hitler did become a god for millions. Rudolf Höss, commander of Auschwitz, stated before his execution in 1947 that he would have gassed and burned his own wife, children, and even himself if only the Führer had commanded it. Much of the nation came under the spell of a man who was hailed as the long-awaited Savior of a people who had become weary of poverty and humiliation.

At one of the Nuremberg rallies, a giant photo of Hitler was captioned with the words "In the beginning was the Word." The Lord's Prayer was changed by some to read, "Our Father Adolf who art in Nuremberg, Hallowed be thy name, the Third Reich come . . ." If you did not say, "Heil Hitler!" when you entered a restaurant or a business establishment, you would not be served.

Millions agreed with Alfred Rosenberg, who said, "Let it happen as it will and must, but I believe in Hitler; above him there hovers a star."[10] Although dictators are usually hated by most, this one was for the most part adored, obeyed, and worshiped.

Secular historians have admitted that Hitler cannot be explained merely as a shrewd politician who appeared in Germany at a time when the nation was ripe for a dictatorship. Allan Bullock, who wrote an extensive biography of Hitler, dutifully listed what Hitler studied in his youth: yoga, hypnotism, astrology, and various other forms of Eastern occultism, yet Bullock sees little connection between these and Hitler's awesome spiritual powers. He confesses, "For my part, the more I learn about Adolf Hitler, the harder I find it to explain and accept what happened. Somehow the causes are inadequate to account for the size of the effects. . . . It is here in the gap between the explanation and the event that the fascination of Hitler's career remains."[11]

ANTICHRIST, AS WE WILL LEARN, WILL MAKE HITLER LOOK AS IF HE HAD PLAYED IN THE MINOR LEAGUES.

Bullock evidently never did discover what that "gap" might be. He did admit that Hitler, to his last days, had an uncanny gift of personal magnetism that defied analysis and adds, "His power to bewitch an audience has been likened to the occult arts of the African Medicineman or the Asiatic Shaman." But Bullock never saw that as the source of Hitler's mysterious power.

The "gap" can only be explained by Hitler's personal acquaintance with satanic powers that enabled him to mesmerize the masses and give Nazism an almost irresistible magnetic attraction. Thousands went to the Nuremberg rallies as skeptics and returned as dedicated worshipers of "the Führer." In short, we cannot understand Nazism without understanding the "religion" of the Third Reich.

What was this new religion? Many of its fundamental beliefs are widely accepted today, especially by those who might not understand the basic unity of all occult religions. And of course, these teachings will be the religion of the future Antichrist. It is a religion of unity, power, hope, and miracles. Someday there will be what Reinhold Kerstan calls an "updated" Führer. Antichrist, as we will learn, will make Hitler look as if he had played in the minor leagues.

We can't help but wonder whether the church was warning people about this satanic occultism that swept Germany. The lie that Christianity can be combined with the esoteric mysticism of other religions is easily believed by those who are ignorant of the biblical warnings about such compromise. The apparent silence of the church about such rebellion is a warning to us who live in an age when these same ideas flourish in our country, albeit in a different form.

THE RELIGION OF NAZISM

Let's consider these teachings in more detail. What were the doctrines of Hitler's new religion? We will recognize these teachings as both very old and very contemporary.

THE TRANSFORMATION OF CONSCIOUSNESS

In the Hofburg Library in Vienna, there is a spear believed by many to be the one used to pierce the side of Christ. One day when Adolf Hitler was in his early twenties, he overheard a tour guide point the spear out to a group of visitors and say, "This spear is shrouded in mystery; whoever unlocks its secrets will rule the world." Later Hitler said that those words changed his whole life.

Hitler soon discovered that many spears vied for the dubious honor of being the one used to smite Christ's side. Nevertheless, he became convinced that the one in the Hofburg Library did have awesome powers for good or evil. He noted that when kings or emperors had it in their possession, they were victorious; when it fell from their possession they lost the battle. Standing before the spear, Hitler made an irreversible vow to follow Satan.

Hitler stared at this object for hours, inviting its hidden powers to invade his soul. He believed that this ancient weapon was a bridge between the world of sense and the world of spirit. He felt as if he had held it in his hands in an earlier century.

Walter Stein, who befriended Hitler in those days, said that Hitler stood before the spear,

> like a man in a trance, a man over whom some dreadful spell had been cast. . . . The very space around him seemed enlivened with some subtle irradiation, a kind of ghostly ectoplasmic light. [He] appeared transformed as if some mighty Spirit now inhabited his very soul, creating

within and around him a kind of evil transformation of its own nature and power.[12]

Standing there in the Hofburg, Dr. Stein said, Hitler experienced a kind of "eclipse of consciousness." When Hitler marched into Vienna, he was convinced that Fate had decreed that he should personally become the possessor of the magical spear that he had gazed upon years before. According to Trevor Ravenscroft, Hitler took the spear from behind the glass, and it became for him a spear of revelation. "It was," Hitler said, "as if I were holding the whole world in my hand."[13]

If this story seems to be unbelievable, we must remember that any object given over to Satan can become the means of entry into the spirit world. Though that particular spear most probably was not the spear used to pierce Christ's side, it was a bridge that kings and emperors used to make contact with Satan. For Hitler it not only symbolized the Roman antagonism toward Christ but also was a path to Luciferic transformation.

The doctrine of the transformation of consciousness, which is as old as paganism, teaches that we can be in touch with nonhuman intelligences from whom we gain wisdom and power. These beings, often referred to today as "masters of wisdom," are available to those who wish to pay the price of initiation. The details vary from culture to culture, but the message is the same: Altered states of consciousness are possible if we are willing to expand our mental horizons and get in touch with "the powers." Quite literally, this is a "new birth," an esoteric experience of enlightenment. To have the experience is to belong to an elite group of initiated ones.

Although mesmerized by Eastern occultism, Hitler was impatient with transcendental meditation and preferred the speedier route of drugs to connect with the spiritual powers. He befriended a used book dealer, Earnest Pretzsche, who introduced him to a psychedelic drug that produced clairvoyant visions and heightened spiritual perceptions. In this way he was empowered to perform the deeds that he believed Fate had decreed.

Even those who knew Hitler from his early days were well aware of his occult powers. August Kubizek, a friend, said, "It was as if another being spoke out of his body. . . . It was not a case of a speaker carried away by his own words. . . . I felt as though he himself listened with astonishment and emotion to what broke forth from him."[14]

After Hitler joined the group that became known as the Nazi party, he was initiated into deeper levels of occult transformation. Through rituals and pacts with demonic forces, he was changed into a man of such awesome power that skeptics regularly became fanatics just by listening to his speeches. And when he finished his harangues, he often would collapse in exhaustion, just like a medium who had been in touch with the netherworld. He needed time to rest and be revived.

Hitler also believed in the Eastern doctrine of reincarnation, a conviction that would serve him well in his attempt to exterminate the Jews (this will be explained in the next chapter). Hitler believed he was the reincarnation of many ancient kings, including Tiberius of Rome.

But even if we grant, as I believe we must, that Hitler was indwelt by an evil spirit(s) or possibly by Satan himself, we are faced with a question: What about his millions of followers? What made them fanatically committed to the dictates of "the Führer"?

Let us remember that a demonic leader is able to unleash spiritual forces that influence others. As Houston Chamberlain, who was the occult adviser to Kaiser Wilhelm II, said, "Hitler is an awakener of souls, the vehicle of Messianic powers." Serving as a satanic channel was especially possible in a country that was already steeped in occultism.

This national obsession with occultism prepared the way for Hitler's meteoric rise to world prominence. Heinrich Himmler's masseur said that the nation was caught up in "the mysticism of a political movement" and in "no country were so many miracles performed, so many ghosts conjured, so many illnesses cured by magnetism, so many horoscopes read."[15] There were telepathy, séances, and spiritual experiences of every sort, which camouflaged Hitler's deceptions. Just as the New Age movement today might well be preparing the world to accept the miracles of Antichrist, so the occultism of Germany made mass deception much more difficult to detect.

Hitler's closest associates were occultists in their own right. Rudolf Hess, who eventually tried to negotiate his own peace terms with the West, spent his remaining days in prison in Berlin until his death in 1987. Though his wife had not seen him in all those years, she claimed that they were never apart, saying, "Telepathy and astrology and his letters keep us together . . . my husband and I are in constant telepathic contact . . . my husband and I receive and send to each other in this way."[16]

Himmler was a dedicated occultist; so were Rosenberg and Goebbels. As the Nazi party grew, it attracted those who belonged to numerous satanic organizations. The inner Nazi circle drew power directly from these hidden forces. But in a nation that was already steeped in occult doctrines, millions of others came under Hitler's magic spell.

We must remember that those who submit themselves to someone who is demonized risk the possibility of personal deception and a bonding influence to their leader. Interestingly, even some who disagreed with Hitler nevertheless came under his aura and supported him anyway. Powerful deceivers can deceive others who then come under varying degrees of demonic control. Given Germany's spiritual vacuum, the nation was almost eager to be deceived.

Of course, Hitler had to pay for his power. No one can be in league with Satan "on the cheap." Rauschning describes a recurring scenario: "He yells for help . . . seized with power that makes him tremble so violently his bed shakes . . . in his bedroom he is muttering. . . . 'It is he! It is he! He's here!' His lips turn blue. . . . He was dripping with sweat. . . . He was given a massage and something to drink. . . . Then all of a sudden he screamed, 'There! Over there in the corner!'"[17]

Antichrist will, of course, also believe in a personal transformation of consciousness. He will be put in touch with nonhuman intelligences, those special powers that will equip him to rule the world. Who his mentors will be, we do not know; but we do know that he will be put through a disciplined, rigorous demonization process. His power will come not from himself but from invisible spiritual forces. "And his power will be mighty, but not by his own power, and . . . he will destroy mighty men and the holy people" (Daniel 8:24). As we learned in the last chapter, Antichrist will not be able to do what he does without the power that has been "given to him."

Many who despise Hitler today, many who pride themselves in condemning Nazism, are actually embracing the same doctrines that made Nazism the powerful force it was in the world. Astute readers will realize that what is popularly called the New Age movement is ancient occultism, or we could call it the spiritual doctrines of Nazism with a friendly American face.

Obviously, not everyone who embraces the doctrines of personal transformation becomes as evil as Hitler. Indeed, a person might experience personal improvement, be more fulfilled, more in touch with himself or herself and more confident of the future. Satan does different things to different people. If you are seeking peace, he will try to give it to you; if you are in need of advice, he will do his best to predict the future and give you secret information through the stars or a fortune-teller. If you are in need of self-confidence or even a miracle, he will try to do that too. In Hitler's case he needed power to rule, and Satan made that available.

The Bible forbids any contact with the spirit world for one good reason: Demons masquerade as angels of light, seeking to deceive as many as they can. Of course, there are "masters," or nonhuman intelligences, waiting for an opportunity to get in touch with human beings. To bring about such a transformation of consciousness is exactly what the Evil One desires.

THE ESSENTIAL DEITY OF MAN

Ever since Adam and Eve believed Satan's promise—that if they ate the fruit of the forbidden tree, they would be like God, knowing good and evil—humans have tried to set up a rival kingdom. To be like God is an awesome thought. Man is intelligent enough to know that he is not the creator, so mankind says, "Yes, I am God, but so is nature; in fact everything is God and God is everything."

Hitler confided to those who were closest to him that he was under orders from higher beings in his unique mission. "I will tell you a secret," he told Rauschning, "I am founding an order. . . . the Man-God, that splendid being will be an object of worship. . . . But there are other stages about which I am not permitted to speak."[18] We can only speculate as to who was forbidding him to reveal more.

After reading his friend Alfred Rosenberg's blasphemous book entitled *The Myth of the Twentieth Century*, Hitler declared, "Creation is not yet at an end. Man is becoming God. . . . Man is God in the making."[19] Joseph Goebbels, his propaganda minister, reveals the hypnotic effect Hitler exerted on him when they first met. "He is the creative instrument of fate and deity. I stand by him deeply shaken . . . recognize him as my leader. . . . He is so deep and mystical, like a prophet of old. With such a man one can conquer the world. . . . My doubts vanish . . . Germany will live! Heil Hitler![20]

In 1941, the historian Benoist-Mechin met Hitler and declared in awe, "His eyes, so strange that at first they were all I saw. . . . [He] had a way of looking at you which drew you to him. . . . You felt a sort of dizziness."[21] Millions who feared him nevertheless admired and worshiped him.

Watch some Hitler newsreels, and the adoration of the crowds is astounding. If the *Heil!* greeting was borrowed from the secret brotherhood of List, the famed Nazi salute was used to invoke the power of earth and soil in the occult organization the Order of the Golden Dawn. In an interview, I heard a woman say that when she shook hands with Hitler, she returned to her hometown to be treated like a "goddess." She had, said one villager, "shaken the hand of the German god."

HITLER SAID THAT A BIG LIE IS MORE EASILY BELIEVED THAN A SMALL ONE. IF SO, THE BIGGEST LIE IS THAT A MAN CAN BE GOD.

Antichrist's goal, like that of Hitler, will be to be worshiped. At the beginning of the Tribulation period, he will make a covenant with Israel, apparently guaranteeing the peaceful existence of that small but significant country. But after three and one half years, he will have enough confidence to go to Jerusalem and break his treaty. He will enter the temple (which will have been rebuilt by that time), desecrate it, and declare himself to be God. Paul describes him as one "who opposes and exalts himself above every so-called god or object of worship, so that he takes his seat in the temple of God, displaying himself as being God" (2 Thessalonians 2:4).

We can smile when gurus tell us today that we are all gods and that we need to simply realize our potential. But the godhood of man, which has always been believed in various forms in the East, is now being accepted in the West too. Just as Germany accepted Hitler because of rampant occultism, so our nation is being prepared for a leader who claims to be god. After all, if we are all little gods, why cannot a charismatic ruler be called the bigger God, the personification of deity?

Just as Hitler suppressed rival worship and practically crushed the church, so Antichrist will destroy all opposition. Christianity and

Judaism will especially be his targets. Before him almost all knees will bow.

Hitler said that a big lie is more easily believed than a small one. If so, the biggest lie is that a man can be God. This new religion will claim to be able to encompass all the others and will combine science and religion. God will be described as an impersonal "force" or "energy." This concept of God will allow for many gods, just as long as Satan orchestrates them all. Eventually we can expect a new theology to arise that will not even attempt to refute Christian doctrine but will simply ignore it.

When you hear someone immersed in the esoteric doctrines of the East say, "I believe we are all gods," you have just heard a satanic creed that is as old as Eden. Those who believe it would probably be surprised to be told that this was the basic premise of Adolf Hitler and an even more powerful coming Prince.

A GLOBAL VISION

What catapulted Hitler to power? The stock market crash of 1929, which triggered economic hardship in Germany, was the catalyst; but without the rage of world conquest burning in his breast, the Third Reich would never have happened. He believed that he would begin a one-thousand-year Reich, or empire, that would eventually span the globe. Since men such as Karl Haushofer accepted the myth that the Germans (Aryans) belonged to a superior race, the nation had every right to extend its empire to dominate the world.

Hitler was able to ignite a spark of optimism in a beleaguered nation. Millions were caught up in the grand idea of a leader with a plan to bring Germany out of its days of humiliation to a day of pride and strength. Even the skeptical preferred to suppress their doubts. As one observer who lived in the era said, "Though I couldn't accept Hitler and knew he was crazy, I wished in my heart that I could be a part of his movement."

Globalism has always been the long-term goal of occult religions. At the Parliament of the World's Religions in Chicago in 1993, six thousand delegates came from all over the world to discuss the need to unite the religions of the world. The assumption was that world hunger, war, and injustice are so staggering that only a unified religion and government can solve these problems. A global ethic was adopted, in which the word *God* does not appear, but the word *Earth* is capitalized throughout. The document says that there cannot be a transformation of earth unless there is a transformation of consciousness.

> In conclusion we appeal to all the inhabitants of this planet. Earth cannot be changed for the better unless the consciousness of individuals is changed. We pledge to work for such transformation in individual and collective consciousness, of the wakening of our spiritual powers. . . . Together we can move mountains.[22]

When people are desperate, they usually seek to unite under the banner of men rather than under the banner of God. Whether in Nazi Germany or in our own day, the Cross is pushed aside in deference to some other flag. To dominate the world is an ambition that does not die easily within the human breast.

AN OBSESSION WITH CONTROL

Every dictator—past, present, and future—is obsessed with the need to keep his subjects in line. Hitler kept the Germans marching to the beat of his drum by threats and brutality. First, by the SA (storm troops) and then by his SS (elite guard), the nation was made to fear rival ideas and disobedience. In a massive swearing-in ceremony in Munich, the SS troops pledged personal allegiance to Hitler. They administered discipline; they intimidated, and they tortured. Anyone who was suspected of being an accomplice to insubordination was ostracized, imprisoned, or eliminated. Hitler was the consummate control fiend.

A friend of mine who served in Hitler's army told me that soldiers came to farmers to ask for clothes for the troops during the bitter Russian campaign of 1941–42. When pressed for a donation, one woman asked angrily, "How long will this continue?" Hours later a car pulled up in front of her house, and she was arrested, never to return.

Through surveillance, wiretaps, spying, and rewarding those who betrayed their friends, Hitler tried to control the citizens of Germany. He had instilled in all of his subordinates the obsessive desire to be obeyed and worshiped. Of course the goal behind all black magic is power, the thirst to wield supreme power over the whole world. In a word, it was the drive to be God. It was Lucifer who said that he would be "like the Most High."

But Hitler did not have the technology to bring every subject of his realm into line. He was bothered that there were some who did not adore him and they were getting away with it! Some who served Hitler with their bodies despised him in their minds. The failed assassination attempts were constant reminders that he was finite, unable to capture the worship he so desperately craved.

THE RELIGION OF A FUTURE REICH

There are reasons that Hitler has often been seen as the prototype of the Antichrist. The Bible predicts that a world ruler will arise in Europe who will promise peace while preparing for war. He will mesmerize the world, demanding the worship of the masses in exchange for the right to buy bread. He, like Hitler, will be indwelt by demonic forces, most likely by Satan himself. The parallels are so striking that Robert Van Kampen in his book *The Sign* says that he believes that the Antichrist will actually be Hitler raised from the dead.[23] Though this supposition is unlikely, it does remind us of the mystical aura that surrounds Hitler's name even today.

Antichrist will fare better than Hitler. Since globalism is already a powerful force in the world, many organizations and leaders will cooperate in solving the problems of this planet. He will win the world to his side. Crying for bread and peace, a desperate world will surrender its personal rights in return for what will eventually be empty promises. He will be first admired, then feared, then worshiped throughout the whole world.

Antichrist will achieve what Hitler only dreamed about. His power to do miracles will be so great that the whole world will marvel as one of his heads appears "as if it had been slain, and his fatal wound was healed" (Revelation 13:3). This may be a satanic attempt to mimic the resurrection of Christ. And it will work because we read that "the whole earth was amazed and followed after the beast."

Of Antichrist we read, "And all who dwell on the earth will worship him, everyone whose name has not been written from the foundation of the world in the book of life of the Lamb who has been slain" (v. 8). Imagine! Hitler received the worship of millions within *one country* of the world. Antichrist will receive the worship of billions in *every country* of the world. Even remote tribes, obscure countries whose names we find difficult to pronounce, will worship him en masse.

Antichrist will find a better way to enforce his control. He will use the economy as his weapon. We read, "And he causes all, the small and the great, and the rich and the poor, and the free men and the slaves, to be given a mark on their right hand, or on their forehead, and he provides that no one should be able to buy or to sell, except the one who has the mark, either the name of the beast or the number of his name" (vv. 16–17).

He will be shrewd enough to understand what Hitler knew so well: People have to eat in order to live. And the words of Satan regarding Job will prove to be true, "All that a man has he will give for his life" (Job 2:4). So an apparatus will be set up to make sure that everyone on earth, willingly or unwillingly, bows before Antichrist.

Erwin Chargaff wrote, "I see the beginning of a new barbarism . . . which tomorrow will be called a new culture. . . . Naziism was but a primitive, brutish and absurd expression of it. But it was a first draft of the so-called scientific or pre-scientific morality that is being prepared in the radiant future."[24]

Though Satan will get what he wants, there is a cloud on the horizon. He knows—just as we do—that his time is short and his coming torment so much greater. Every time he wins, he actually loses, for God has the final say. The charade will be over, and Satan will be exposed for who he really is—a loser, a loser for all eternity.

The description of the judgment of Hitler, Antichrist, and all who refuse to follow God is described in Revelation 20:10: "And the devil who deceived them was thrown into the lake of fire and brimstone, where the beast and the false prophet are also; and they will be tormented day and night forever and ever."

Since this judgment is still future, we must ask: Where is Hitler today? He committed suicide in his bunker in Berlin. As instructed, his body was badly burned, possibly beyond recognition. But his soul survived the gunshot wound and the flames. He is conscious today; his memory is clearer than it was at a noonday rally in Nuremberg. His emotions are fully aware; he feels the torment of his evil deeds. His will, however, remains unbowed; his resolve to oppose God is firm (even if he did change his mind, it would not affect his eternal destiny).

A 1931 picture of Adolf Hitler leaving church. Two years later Hitler became chancellor and moved to control the German churches. He even distributed this photograph as part of his effort to gain support.

Christ pulled back the curtain and allowed us to look into Hades, the place where the souls of unbelievers await the final judgment. A certain rich man was in torment and cried out, "Father Abraham, have mercy on me, and send Lazarus, that he may dip the tip of his finger in water and cool off my tongue; for I am in agony in this flame" (Luke 16:24). Hitler also feels that flame today. It's a preview of what is to come.

Eventually, Hitler will also be judged and thrown into the lake of fire along with the dragon, beast, and false prophet. All demonic religion will have been shown to be false, deceptive, and weak. And every tongue will confess that Christ is Lord to the glory of God the Father. God will have proven that man cannot rule himself; all attempts to take the scepter from the Almighty were futile and foolish.

A WARNING TO THE CHURCH

From my study I have concluded that the church in Germany appeared to be too preoccupied with the problems of the nation to see what was happening before its eyes. The religion of blood and soil had replaced the religion of humility and prayer. Though burdened with unemployment and the physical hardship of its dejected people, the church, for the most part, still refused to repent and turn wholly to God.

THE CHURCH STOOD POISED BETWEEN TWO CROSSES, WANTING TO BE LOYAL TO BOTH BUT LEARNING THAT NEITHER CROSS COULD TOLERATE THE OTHER.

Popular German culture, with its myths about race and occultism, thrived in place of sound Bible teaching and prayer. The church overlooked the fact that the fight against Nazism was essentially not political but spiritual. *The church mistook the temporal benefits of the swastika for the spiritual benefits of the cross of Christ.* Wanting to believe that Hitler was the answer, it forgot what the really important questions were.

Paul had warned the elders in Ephesus, "Be on guard for yourselves and for all the flock, among which the Holy Spirit has made you overseers, to shepherd the church of God which He purchased with His own blood. I know that after my departure savage wolves will come in among you, not sparing the flock" (Acts 20:28–29). Wolves, we shall learn, had entered the German flocks. The church stood poised between two crosses, wanting to be loyal to both but learning that neither cross could tolerate the other. *The church made peace with an enemy with which it should have been at war.* Called to warn and protect, it tolerated, then saluted, then submitted.

Heinrich Heine was right: When the cross of Christ was broken, evil burst forth in all of its fury. No one felt the onslaught more than the Jews, who were targeted by Hitler's "final solution." Regrettably, even here the church simply did not live up to its high calling.

Antichrist will have his extermination program too, but Christ, the consummate Jew, the Lion of the tribe of Judah, will not let His people be wiped out. Christ's cross will, in the end, destroy any other.

We now turn to this puzzling, yet intriguing, story.

CHAPTER FOUR

THE ANTI-SEMITISM
OF THE THIRD REICH

I do not look upon Jews as animals, they are further removed from animals than we are. . . . Therefore it is not a crime to exterminate them, since they do not belong to humanity at all."[1]

Thus did Adolf Hitler create new laws that would remove the Jews from their status as persons. With his declaration that they were beneath the animals, Heinrich Himmler got the green light to use his SS troops to exterminate them. The SS were then free to kill without breaking laws; they were free to exterminate without committing murder. There would be no trials for poisoning vermin; the land must be cleansed of filth so that it might be peopled with those who have human blood flowing through their veins.

With this verbal sleight of hand, the man who starved children but called it "putting them on a low calorie diet" now killed Jews and called it "cleansing the polluted land." Just as with the abortionist who calls a pre-born infant a "product of conception," so language is craftily manipulated by those who wish to desensitize the conscience and promote humanistic values. If evil is called good, then it becomes good—just ask Adolf Hitler.

The Third Reich cannot be understood apart from the doctrine of race, the belief that only through a pure bloodline can humanity achieve its rightful godhood. Hitler cynically blended the racism of composer Richard Wagner and the evolutionary theory of Charles Darwin with the blood myths of Eastern occultism. He forged a doctrine that would give him permission to vent his rage against the Jews with a plan to exterminate them from the face of the earth.

"Whoever wants to understand National Socialist Germany must know Wagner," Hitler used to say. Wagner, with his operas that reveled in German heroes and wars with pagan gods and demons, was a rabid anti-Semite. This man of staggering genius claimed to have had a revelation that Jesus Christ had been born of Aryan (German) stock. This was not the Jewish Christ of the New Testament, but a Christ who shed Aryan blood and would lead Germany back to the greatness that was her right.[2] In his *Nibelungenlied* (Song of the Nibelungs), Wagner called for an awakening of the German *Volk* (people). And in the grand finale called *Göotterdämmerung* (Twilight of the Gods), he dramatized the conflict by which this awakened Germany would rule. Wagner uttered the term "final solution" long before it became Hitler's official policy.

We should note in passing that there have been many christs throughout history. Even in the New Testament, John warns about a number of antichrists in his day (1 John 2:18). Paul condemned those who preach "another Jesus" (2 Corinthians 11:4) and another gospel, declaring that such should "be accursed" (Galatians 1:9). Wagner was actually a worshiper of Lucifer under the guise of an Aryan Christ who passionately hated the Jews. Little wonder that Hitler adored Wagner and, even as the Third Reich was coming to an end, often reminisced about the effect Wagner had on his life.

Hitler also accepted Charles Darwin's theory of "the survival of the fittest" and asserted that man had every right to be "as cruel as nature." Detailed lectures were given in schools and to SS troops to prove the inferiority of the Jews. Aryan skulls were compared with those of Jewish ancestry to prove on a scientific basis that the latter were hopelessly inferior. Only the "fittest" had the right to survive.

No event in modern history has caused as much reflection as the Holocaust. The sheer enormity of the numbers and the flagrant, wanton cruelty stagger the sober imagination. Those of us who have visited concentration camps in Europe have for a fleeting moment tried to absorb the horror. But I, at least, have found my resources taxed to the breaking point trying to fathom what seems to be unfathomable.

The Holocaust museums in Israel and Washington, D.C., confront us with the scope of the crimes committed, but when we leave them we still feel we have not done justice to this part of world history.

What brings the Holocaust home to me are the personal stories: the letter I read in a museum in Buchenwald, a letter from a mother to her son, telling him that she is anxiously awaiting his return, not knowing that he had already been brutally murdered. The picture of a child with a crust of bread, telling a guard he is keeping his special treasure for "mommy," unaware that he would never see her again. The photographs of guards beating gaunt inmates who, though virtually naked, were forced to carry stones in winter weather. And then the rows of children's shoes, a reminder of the thousands of little ones tortured to death with demonic vengeance.

Talk to Jewish people today, and many of them will tell you that there are no advantages to being chosen. The nonchosen, for all of their trials, have appeared to be more blessed. The chosen appear to be the cursed. With the honor of being singled out by God for blessing has come centuries of tears and persecution. And, as we shall see, there is more to come.

Whether the Jews like it or not, and whether we Gentiles like it or not, the Jewish people are chosen indeed. Listen to the words of God Himself: "For you are a holy people to the Lord your God; the Lord your God has chosen you to be a people for His own possession out of all the peoples who are on the face of the earth" (Deuteronomy 7:6). The Jews, despite their faults, are the nation God chose through which to bless the world. Abraham was a Gentile when God came to him, told him to leave his family, and said to him, "And I will make you a great nation, and I will bless you, and make your name great; and so you shall be a blessing; and I will bless those who bless you, and the one who curses you I will curse. And in you all the families of the earth shall be blessed" (Genesis 12:2–3).

God's covenant with Abraham is shown to be unconditional; that is, it is wholly dependent on the faithfulness of God. In Genesis 15 the covenant is ratified when God alone walks between the pieces of symmetrical flesh while Abraham sleeps. Thus God was "swearing by Himself" that the terms of the agreement would be fulfilled (Genesis 15:12–21). Jacob, a descendant of Abraham, had twelve sons, one of whom was Judah from whose name the word *Jew* was derived.

Gentiles inherit the blessing only because of God's graciousness; we are grafted into the "olive tree," to use Paul's analogy. Israel failed to accept God's Messiah, so we Gentiles are the beneficiaries of God's love and affection. But God isn't finished with Israel. Many of us believe that in the end He will still fulfill His covenant to them as a nation.

Before we take a tour of four phases of Jewish persecution, we must pause to be wary of those who would misuse this terrible tragedy to further their own agendas. In America the radical homosexual community has often perpetrated the story that homosexuals were among the victims of Hitler's Holocaust. Thus, those who are opposed to the imposition of gay rights in society are likened to Hitler who viciously persecuted his victims. The link between the emotionally charged image of Hitler and those who would oppose special laws that favor homosexuals is an artificial one, but it is tempting to exploit the connection.

Gay rights activists have held rallies at the museums in Israel and Washington, protesting that they were overlooked in the memorials. This tactic follows the strategy proposed in a homosexual paper, which advised that gays should "portray themselves as victims, not aggressive challengers. In any campaign to win over the public," the authors contended, "gays must be cast as victims in need of protection so that straights will be inclined by reflex to assume the role of protector."[3]

Extensive research by Kevin E. Abrams has revealed that, whereas homosexuals were put into the death camps, they were never targeted for extermination as a class and were treated far better than most other concentration camp victims. Two years after Hitler's victory, the term "unnatural" was purged from the definition of homosexuality in the German Criminal Code. Even gay historian Jonathan Katz reports that, though police repeatedly apprehended homosexual actors and artists engaged in sodomy, they were not to be arrested.

It would have been strange indeed if the Nazis had singled out homosexuals for special persecution since the movement itself was rampant with various kinds of sexual perversion. Historian Samuel Igra states that Hitler's initial Brownshirts began as an exclusive homosexual and bisexual organization. Hitler's personal secretary, Rudolf Hess, was a bisexual known in homosexual circles as "Fräulein Anna." Homosexuality was rampant in Hitler's inner circle as well as in the SS, as boys were rounded up from the Hitler Youth to participate

Dining hall in the barracks of the *Leibstandarte,* Hitler's SS bodyguard. The legend beneath the eagle reads "The will of the Führer remains our faith."

in sexual orgies.[4] Of course, Hitler railed against homosexuals, just as he did against occultists, though he himself was a dedicated satanist.

It would be a mistake to think that only Jews died in the concentration camps. Hitler used torture chambers for anyone whom he deemed an enemy. Though the vast majority of those who died were Jews, they were joined by an assortment of Communists, intellectuals, religious leaders, and anyone else whom the SS troops didn't like. Hundreds of thousands of Soviets and Poles were put to death along with political prisoners from other nationalities. The extermination of the Jews, however, was Hitler's most cherished goal. In keeping with Wagner's dream, it was his "final solution."

A CROSS LIES AGAINST A BLACK BACKGROUND TO COMMEMORATE THE SAD FACT THAT MILLIONS OF JEWS HAD SUFFERED UNDER THE VERY CROSS THAT WAS TO BE A SYMBOL OF FORGIVENESS AND RECONCILIATION.

In the next few pages we will explore that hatred for the Jews; though perfected by Hitler, it did not begin with him. Often Christians are impatient with Jews because of their outright rejection of Christ. It is difficult for Gentiles to understand why many Jewish people dismiss Christ out of hand and are often (though not always) closed off to any serious discussion of Him as the Messiah. As Gentiles, we forget that Christ is thought of as an enemy of the Jews. A Jewish woman told some of us at a Bible study that when she was searching for God she feared studying the New Testament in case it turned out to be true. She often prayed, "O God, turn out to be anybody but Jesus!"

Join me as we tour four phases of Jewish history that will culminate with the return of Christ. Be prepared for some surprises along the way.

CHRISTIANITY AND JUDAISM

Come with me to the German town of Wittenberg, made famous by the reformer Martin Luther. When we enter the town, we see the imposing Castle Church where Luther nailed his ninety-five theses.

There within the church, he is buried just under the pulpit, about fifteen feet from his friend Melanchton.

When we walk across the town square, we come to the town church where Luther preached the gospel to the common people of Wittenberg. But if you walk around to the back of the church and look up at the point where the roof and wall meet, you will see the sandstone relief of a pig, a sculpture perhaps three feet long and eighteen inches high.

This pig, as I learned while leading a tour to the sites of the Reformation, is a *Judensau* (a "Jewish sow") erected to spite the Jews and commemorate their expulsion from Wittenberg in 1305. The Hebrew inscription reads, *"Rabine Schem Ha Mphoras,"* which means, "Great is the name of the one who is blessed." This phrase was used by the Jews to refer to God since they believed that His name should not even be pronounced. Now these words sarcastically refer to them, contemptuously linking them to a pig, an animal regarded by them as being most unholy!

Our tour group looked up with disgust to think that such a symbol of hatred was placed on a Christian church. Our sadness dissipated slightly when we saw a memorial on the ground dated 1988 that was, in effect, an apology for what had happened so many centuries ago. A cross lies against a black background to commemorate the sad fact that millions of Jews had suffered under the very cross that was to be a symbol of forgiveness and reconciliation. A translation of the inscription reads:

> The true name of God
> The maligned, "Schem Ha Mphoras"
> Which the Jews even before the dawn of Christianity
> Regard as most inexpressibly holy
> This name died within six million Jews
> Under the symbol of a cross.

Psalm 130:1 is inscribed, "Out of the depths I have cried unto Thee, O Lord." Thus fifty years after the *Kristallnacht* (Crystal Night, so named because of the glass shattered when Jewish shops throughout Germany were pillaged), the church humbly recognized its sin in mocking and persecuting the Jews.

But what about Luther himself? William Shirer in his classic, *The Rise and Fall of the Third Reich,* calls the Great Reformer a "passionate anti-Semite." Luther called the Jews "venomous," "bitter worms," and "disgusting vermin." In 1543, near the end of his life, he wrote three tracts against the Jews. Throughout four centuries, his words have often been quoted by Jews as proof that Christ could not be their friend. Listen to Luther's advice as to how to treat them.

> First, to set fire to their synagogues or schools and to bury and cover with dirt whatever will not burn, so that no man will ever again see stone or cinder of them. This is to be done in honor of our Lord and Christendom. . . . Second, I advise that their houses also be razed and destroyed. . . . Third, I advise that all their prayer books and Talmudic writings, in which such idolatry, lies, cursing, and blasphemy are taught, be taken from them. Fourth, I advise that their rabbis be forbidden to teach henceforth on pain of loss of life and limb. Fifth, I advise that safe-conduct on the highways be abolished completely for the Jews. . . . Sixth, I advise that usury be prohibited to them, and that all cash and treasure of silver and gold be taken from them and put aside for safekeeping.[5]

Luther, how could you?

In *Mein Kampf,* Hitler commended Luther as a great reformer who was worthy to be classed with Frederick the Great and Richard Wagner. But, unfortunately, Hitler did not admire Luther because he uncovered the gospel and proclaimed salvation through Christ alone by faith alone. Rather, he saw him as a man of courage who withstood the church and, no doubt, as one who hated the Jews. But we can be quite sure that if Luther had lived in Hitler's day he not only would have opposed Hitler's racially motivated hatred of the Jews but would have also condemned the Führer as Antichrist. Too bad that Hitler did not see the other side to Luther, a man who, for all of his faults, did understand the meaning of Christ's cross. Hitler understood only the meaning of his own.

In Luther's last days, when the irritability of age and disease took over, he said many things that would have been best left unsaid. Whether it was regarding the papacy or the Anabaptists or the Jews, Luther always spoke in colorful, condemning language.

Needless to say, his comments are despicable and anti-Christian. But we owe it to him to understand the context of his remarks. Here are some words he wrote at an earlier time when he blamed the unbelief of the Jews on the failures of medieval Christianity. We wish he had repeated these comments at the end of his life: "We must indeed with prayer and the fear of God before our eyes exercise a keen compassion towards them [the Jews] and seek to save some of them from the flames. Avenge ourselves we dare not. Vengeance a thousand times more than we can wish them is theirs already."[6]

Why the change of heart? Because Luther was incredibly naive. He actually thought that once he had uncovered the gospel the Jews would accept Christ as Messiah en masse. When they gave no evidence of turning toward Christianity, he turned against them in anger.

Inexcusable as his remarks were, we must bear two things in mind. First, his animosity was *religious,* not *racial.* There is nothing in his writings about the purity of blood, but rather the purity of doctrine. The fact that the Jews rejected Christ made him angry. As for his comments about their wealth, he believed that it had been illegally obtained through usury and thus should be confiscated and put in a fund for "believing Jews." But at root was the medieval notion that it was the responsibility of the church to hate those who hated Christ. The Jews—the "Christ killers"—thus became the target of anger and persecution.

Second, we must bear in mind that Luther lived at a time when freedom of religion was thought to be contrary to the mandate that the earth should be governed according to the truth of the Bible. Thus, there was no freedom of religion as we know it in America. The Catholics persecuted the Protestants and, whenever possible, the Protestants returned the favor. Heretics were burned at the stake or drowned, and the Jews were perceived as the supreme "heretics."

In lashing out against the Jews, Luther was following in the footsteps of other famous Christian leaders. Justin Martyr, in his *Dialogues with Trypho,* wrote that Jewish misfortunes were divine punishment and "tribulations were justly imposed on you for you have murdered the Just One."

Augustine accused the Jews of being guilty of Christ's blood and as being "cursed by the Church." John Chrysostom in 386–87 delivered eight messages degrading the Jewish religion and customs. "God always hated the Jews," he preached. "It is incumbent on all Christians to hate the Jews." In the Middle Ages Jews were murdered by the crusaders en route to the Holy Land.

You probably get the picture. No wonder Jewish people today are kept from serious investigation of the merits of Christ and pray, "O God, turn out to be anybody but Jesus!" They believe that to accept

Christ as the Messiah is not only to deny the Jewish religion, but to deny their heritage, family, and culture. To accept Christ is to embrace an enemy.

A *Chicago Tribune* headline of November 14, 1994, read: "Lutherans Publicly Repudiate Founder." Several hundred Lutherans from the Chicago area had gathered to renounce Martin Luther's anti-Semitic writings. Led by the bishop of the Evangelical Lutheran Church of America, they walked to a nearby synagogue for a joint ceremony to commemorate the declaration of repudiation. "We share in the guilt of those who, bearing the name Martin Luther, slandered and defamed the Jewish people. . . . Whether [it is we] ourselves speaking and killing or standing silent while others vilified and killed, we crucify our Lord anew," the pastor said.

We must commend the ELCA for the courage to make this overture to the Jewish community. Virtually every Jewish person I have spoken to has quoted Luther's remarks to me as one more reason why he or she cannot accept Christianity. We owe it to the Jewish people to apologize for what has been said and done to them in the name of Christ. We are called to love the Jews, to recognize them as God's chosen people and, whatever their faults, to see them as loved by God.

I can do no better than to quote Luther in the days when he spoke more like a Christian: "If some of them [the Jews] should prove stiff-necked, what of it? After all, we ourselves are not all good Christians either." We can only imagine how different the attitude of the Jews might have been if these quotations had been allowed to stand alone and if Luther had proclaimed, "Whoever is anti-Jewish is anti-Christian."

We owe a debt to the Jews that we can never repay. The Bible we hold in our hands is a Jewish book, for as Paul said, "they were entrusted with the oracles of God" (Romans 3:2). And they have given to us a Savior, their Messiah, who has washed us from our sins in His own blood.

For that we say thank you.

JUDAISM AND NAZISM

With Nazism, hatred of the Jews took a new twist. Rather than religious persecution, a new persecution arose, based on a doctrine of race or blood. Theories about racial stratification and blood were rife in Germany long before Hitler rose to power, but he is remembered as the one who used them in a vain attempt to found an empire.

THE MYTH OF RACIAL PURITY

One of the most interesting contributors to the myth of racial superiority was Houston Chamberlain, nephew of Sir Neville Chamberlain. At the age of twenty-seven he moved to Germany, became the son-in-law of composer Richard Wagner, and published a book entitled *The Foundations of the Nineteenth Century,* which rocketed him to fame. I checked this two-volume set out of the library and found his writings to be ponderous, repetitious, and fanciful.

In his book he combined Wagner's theory of the Aryan master race with Nietzsche's theory of the superrace. Chamberlain believed that a "higher race" could be bred; in fact, it already existed in the people of Prussia (the powerful state that unified the rest of the German-speaking peoples). "Just as a pearl can be grown through the medium of artificial stimulation, so the German mind must guide the Aryan peoples to racial supremacy and world domination."[7]

Of Christ, Chamberlain wrote that which could only delight his famous father-in-law's heart: "Whoever claimed that Jesus was a Jew was either stupid or telling a lie. . . . Jesus was not a Jew. He was an Aryan." Christianity, he said, could only be appreciated by the Aryan race. And this race did not lose its superiority by natural law but could be further strengthened by proper breeding.

Even Chamberlain was unprepared for the amazing reception the book received. Soon he became the private soothsayer to Kaiser Wilhelm II, who was the leader of Germany during World War I. The Kaiser told him, "It was God who sent your book to the German people and you personally to me."[8]

Chamberlain reported that he was driven by demons and that most of his writing was done in a trance. He said that he never knew when his soul would be seized by spirits who drove him in his writing. Sometimes he would become a medium and communicate with the dead from whom he would receive messages. He apparently did not realize that these personalities were nonhuman; like all mediums he was in contact with evil spirits who purported to be the personalities of the deceased.

When Germany was defeated in World War I, Chamberlain was dumbfounded and bitterly disappointed. After all, it was he who had

The Führer and Field Marshal Hermann Göring tour one of the Sudetenland towns as Germany begins to occupy the Sudetenland in Czechoslovakia.

encouraged Kaiser Wilhelm II to go to war with the assurance that the Aryan race was destined to win. But years later when Chamberlain met Hitler, he was in awe. Chamberlain wrote to him the next day, "My faith in Germanism has not wavered for an instant. . . . With one stroke you have transformed the state of my soul. That in the hour of her deepest need Germany has given birth to a Hitler proves her vitality; may God protect you!"[9] He helped convince Hitler that achieving a new race could be a political goal. This theory of blood became the cornerstone of Hitler's Third Reich.

These theories did not originate with Chamberlain, but they are as old as pagan mythology. Once upon a time, the legend goes, there was a place called Atlantis, which passed through an age of seven epochs in which subraces developed. The superior race became a divine/human hybrid; they were a sort of God-man. When the superior race left Atlantis, they were led to Tibet and India. Thus there began a superrace that had magical powers, and even spirits would obey their commands. But only those of Aryan blood would be sensitive to this cosmic power. Inferior races would not be a part of the coming mutations.

You will recognize this as the basis for the caste system in India. Hinduism asserts that there are four castes, and beneath them are the untouchables, those subhumans whose Karma decreed that they would be denied the dignity afforded human beings. Those born into the lower rungs of the caste system exist only to serve those above them. The lower ones have no rights but must simply endure their fate with as much tranquillity as they can muster. No wonder Mahatma Gandhi nearly starved himself to death in opposition to the British who wanted to give the untouchables representation in the Indian parliament. Subhumans didn't deserve such rights!

There are three essentials of the caste system. First, your place in society is determined by birth (blood), and there is nothing that can be done in this life to change it. No one moves up the ladder in this life; the inferior races remain such throughout this phase of their existence. Second, the only hope of salvation is that one be reincarnated, that is, that one die and be recycled into a higher form of existence. Third, one's lot in this life and the life to come is determined by the impersonal law of Karma, which doles out favors or judgments in accordance with one's performance in a previous existence.

Hitler was fascinated by Hinduism and other expressions of occultism. The Hindu idea of a master Aryan race taking control of those who are inferior had already been forming in his mind. We have already learned that he borrowed the swastika from Guido von List, but it originated in India where it has been revered for eight thousand years.

Chamberlain confirmed Hitler's racial notions and energized him with the vision of a master race of Germanic people. Hitler was consumed with the challenge of world domination. He had already accepted the Hindu notion that one's fate is determined by blood, but he now believed that one could shorten the process of developing a master race by exterminating those who were inferior. In Hitler's mind, the very existence of the subhuman races hindered the development of the master race.

THE TRAINING OF THE SS

If anyone was more mesmerized by Hinduism than Hitler, it was Heinrich Himmler, the head of the dreaded SS. He communicated regularly with personalities of the past and claimed that he himself was the reincarnation of the tenth-century German king Heinrich I the Fowler, with whom he had frequent communication. He was obsessed with a secret medieval society called the Order of the Teutonic Knights, whose teachings he used to form the elite SS guard.

Himmler said that he did not act without reference to the Hindu writings. He was particularly fond of the Bhagavad-Gita and the Hindu Arthasastra, which described a system of control and espionage that he found valuable in his role as head of the SS. He said that Karma required only that one do his duty without regard to consequences; he accepted the Eastern notion that one should become detached from this world through meditation.[10]

Himmler was faced with the problem of how to take decent German young men and deaden their consciences so that they would be willing to perform ghastly deeds of cruelty. Both Hitler and Himmler believed that each of the SS troops had to perform some deed that violated his conscience and sense of decency. Only when they did what others found to be reprehensible would they break away from their old values. The conscience had to be deadened through these acts of barbarism; that would serve the dual purpose of cutting the recruit off from his past ties, his family and friends, and of bonding him to his new peers and his leader. The break would be so complete that he could never go back. An act of torture or murder would unite him with blood brothers who had crossed the same line, felt the same numbness, and sworn themselves to uphold the same cause.

The SS organization would then become their family, their source of unity and affirmation, their *Gemeinschaft* (community or assembly). At all costs, one should never be left alone but must constantly be active as a vital part of the larger group, a group that was beyond good and evil. The SS leader became the father the boy never had. The group was beyond criticism; there could be rage without guilt, irrational torture without responsibility. The unity and obedience of the group fostered the fantasy of omnipotence, the illusion that they were all a part of a grand cause.[11]

To transform the men into nonthinking, unfeeling machines, Himmler needed to indoctrinate them into a secret society of their own. He assured them that a master race was developing, and if the inferior races stood in their way the scientific belief in "the survival of the fittest" dictated that these races had to be exterminated. Indeed,

SS troops proudly parade through Berlin, lifting their legs high in the familiar "goose step."

they were on a "divine mission" to create a new man and could only do so if these subhumans were prevented from multiplying and populating the earth. To refuse an order was not even to enter their minds. The mystical rituals bonded them to the conviction that they were all members of the elect.

The Nazis proved that ordinary people, if controlled with rigid discipline and the power of mass psychology, can be induced to carry out the most brutal and destructive crime the human mind can devise. Researchers have concluded that Hitler's SS troops were no different psychologically from the rest of humanity. George Kren and Leon Rappoport write, "Our judgment is that the overwhelming majority of the S.S. men, leaders as well as rank and file, would have easily passed all the psychiatric tests ordinarily given to army recruits or Kansas City Policemen."[12]

The SS themselves were convinced that they were the first stage of the superman mutation. The master race was being bred. With the undesirables out of the way, the pace would quicken and a transformation of humanity would accelerate. In order to join the SS, they had to trace their Aryan blood back three generations. Troops also had to meet certain physical qualifications, and each member knew that to betray his oath of loyalty to Hitler meant the destruction of himself and his family. They were embarking on a cause that was so noble that they should suspend their natural judgment; they were on the cutting edge of creating a new society. The goal was to become indifferent to sorrow or guilt, even when expected to kill children. They were to become as hard as their leaders.

THE CHRISTIAN CROSS DEMANDED THE BLOOD OF CHRIST; THE SWASTIKA DEMANDED THE BLOOD OF THE JEWISH NATION.

The group gave each man a feeling that he was needed, and together their unit was beyond criticism. The human will was transcended; all self-identity was lost in the larger cause. The troops could say with Hermann Göring, "I have no conscience! Adolf Hitler is my conscience!" or, "It is not I who live, but the Führer who lives in me."

Himmler echoed the words of Hitler when speaking of the Jews, "They do not belong to the same species but only imitate humans . . . they are as far removed from us as animals are from humans."[13] His troops sang a song together as they marched:

> Sharpen the long knives
> On the pavement stone
> Sink the knives into
> Jewish flesh and bone
> Let the blood flow freely.

Himmler also believed in the theory of reincarnation and claimed that his troops were actually doing the occupants of the concentration camps a favor by exterminating them. After death, these subhumans would obtain salvation of sorts when they reappeared in their next cycle of existence. The SS were simply helping these vermin get on with their own Karma and evolutionary transformation.

Indeed, those who were beaten and starved in the death camps were not the real victims; the Nazis themselves were victims, needing to make great sacrifices for the cause of the master race! Over and over Himmler referred to the work of his SS men in concentration camps as sacrifice. It was as though they suffered more than the people whom they tortured. "To have stuck it out," he said to his officers, "and at the same time to have remained decent fellows, that is what has made us hard. This is a page of glory in our history which has never been written and is never to be written."[14] He had accepted the Eastern occult idea that one must be detached from one's acts, and what seems monstrous to others is purifying to the wise. What is called reality was illusionary.

The brainwashing the troops received helps explain how the SS troops could perform monstrous acts of cruelty and yet return home for Christmas and attend church and still think of themselves as good Christians. They were not murderers; they were men who were building a race of supermen and helping the inferior people get on with their evolutionary journey. Thanks to Karma everyone was simply getting what he/she deserved. To quote Himmler, they were still "decent fellows."

Yet there is more to the story. The Bible teaches that we are redeemed by the blood of Christ, who died that we might be saved. The Old Testament is clear that without the shedding of blood there is no remission of sins. When we pause to think about it, we can see that the Hindu-Aryan mysticism was a demonic counterpart to this teaching. The inferior "beings" in the concentration camps were shedding their blood to "purify" the blood of the Aryan race. Thus the Jews were actually being offered as sacrifices to the Aryan gods. *The Christian cross demanded the blood of Christ; the swastika demanded the blood of the Jewish nation.*

Of course Hindus, I'm sure, would want to distance themselves from the atrocities of the Third Reich. However, many of them do recognize that Hitler was an "avatar," that is, a god who has been incarnated on earth to punish the British for their enslavement of India in the last century. To quote the words of Swami Svatantrananda, "Whatever you may say of him, Hitler was a mahatma, almost like an avatar. He did not eat meat, he did not have intercourse with women, he never even married, and he was the visual incarnation of Aryan polity."[15]

I want to make clear that I am not blaming Hinduism for what happened in Nazi Germany. Hitler and his cronies are accountable to God for their actions, and we must take Hindu leaders seriously when they denounce the excesses of the Third Reich. What cannot be denied, however, is the fact that Hindu doctrines were believed by the leaders of the SS and helped justify the "final solution." The cruel doctrine of the caste system, based on mythical ideas about blood, became even crueler under Hitler's leadership.

THE MYTH OF SELECTIVE PERSONHOOD

Though we are critical of Hitler for removing the Jews from the category of personhood, we who live in America should not forget that we have our own word games; a slick legal maneuver of our Supreme Court arbitrarily asserts that a certain category of persons can be denied the rights of personhood. Pre-born babies are not human, the Court said, and therefore do not deserve constitutional protection. Millions of infants have been sacrificed to the gods of immorality and convenience with the full protection of the law. Unfortunately those who shout that they are "pro-choice" deny choice to the very person who has the most at stake.

The arbitrary morality of the Supreme Court decision of 1973 is not the first time that people have been classified as nonpersons by the High Court. Dred Scott was a black slave who served an army surgeon named John Emerson. When Emerson was stationed in regions where slavery was prohibited, Scott sued for freedom. How could he be legally bound as a slave in places where slavery was illegal?

Much to its shame, the Supreme Court ruled that blacks were not intended to be included as citizens of the United States and therefore could not expect to have constitutional rights. Blacks were described as "beings of an inferior order," and the slave "was bought and sold and treated as an ordinary article of merchandise and traffic whenever a profit could be made by it."[16]

After the Civil War, Congress approved a constitutional amendment that guaranteed rights to "all persons." We applaud that decision, of course, but are grieved that another class of human beings has since been denied legal protection. When we no longer protect the weakest among us, we display a heartlessness that grieves the heart of God. We must repent of our own silent "holocaust" in which five thousand tiny victims lose their lives every day.

JUDAISM AND ANTICHRIST

Hitler's "final solution" was not final. God preserved a remnant of the Jews, established Israel as a state, and today is calling many Jews to faith in Christ, their Messiah. In the end, He shall prove that not one word spoken through the prophets will be neglected. His chosen ones shall yet flourish.

But another holocaust lies ahead.

What sinister motives lay behind Hitler's fanatical hatred of the Jews? In Revelation 12, the mystery of why the Jews have suffered so much becomes plain. The nation is symbolically represented as a persecuted woman who encounters a dragon. When she is with child, the dragon stands by to kill her offspring. Here the hatred against the Jews is unmasked for what it is: It is the direct work of Satan who wants to exterminate the Jews so that God will be found a liar, unable to fulfill His promises.

Behind the hatred of ancient king Herod, behind those Christian leaders whose anger was a stumbling block to the Jewish nation, and behind Hitler's "final solution" is the direct activity of Satan, who is represented in this passage as "the dragon." The story skips to the middle of the coming Tribulation period when the dragon makes one more attempt at his "final solution." He seeks to entrap the woman, but she is given the wings of an eagle that she might fly away; the dragon comes after her with a flood of hatred and warfare in an attempt to kill her once and for all.

> And the serpent poured water like a river out of his mouth after the woman, so that he might cause her to be swept away with the flood. And the earth helped the woman, and the earth opened its mouth and drank up the river which the dragon poured out of his mouth. And the dragon was enraged with the woman, and went off to make war with the rest of her offspring, who keep the commandments of God and hold to the testimony of Jesus. (Revelation 12:15–17)

Notice that God again will do in the future what He did during Hitler's Holocaust: He preserves the woman (the nation) even when it looks as if she will be swallowed up in a river of anti-Semitism. God prepares a place for her; she is preserved, because there are still some promises to the Jewish nation that have to be fulfilled. God lets the dragon go just so far; so far, in fact, that the nation loses hope. But in the end, God is still there.

Many Israelites will again question the faithfulness of God during the period of coming Tribulation. The nation will despair, unaware that a final deliverance from the dragon is just around the corner. Those Jews who believe on Christ will overcome the dragon "because of the blood of the Lamb and because of the word of their testimony, and they did not love their life even to death" (Revelation 12:11).

Thankfully, this final holocaust will come to an end.

JUDAISM AND CHRIST

Just when the nations of the earth have surrounded Jerusalem and appear to be on the verge of exterminating the city and its people, all eyes shift to the Mount of Olives. Christ personally arrives to defend His people and the city of Jerusalem.

Zechariah pictures it: "And in that day His feet will stand on the Mount of Olives, which is in front of Jerusalem on the east; and the Mount of Olives will be split in its middle from east to west by a very large valley, so that half of the mountain will move toward the north and the other half toward the south" (14:4).

At that time, Israel as a nation will recognize Christ to be her Messiah. Again, Zechariah predicts that the Holy Spirit will be poured out upon them, "so that they will look on Me whom they have pierced; and they will mourn for Him, as one mourns for an only son, and they will weep bitterly over Him, like the bitter weeping over a first-born" (12:10).

Just as Joseph revealed himself to his brothers, so Christ will reveal Himself to His kinsmen, the Jews. The weeping will be both of sadness and joy: sadness that it took so long for the reconciliation to take place; joy for the fact that the longing of the Jews is finally fulfilled for the Messiah has arrived.

Paul put it this way, "And thus all Israel will be saved; just as it is written, 'The Deliverer will come from Zion, He will remove ungodliness from Jacob. And this is My covenant with them, when I take away their sins'" (Romans 11:26–27). Virtually the entire nation living at the time of Christ's return will be spared physically and saved spiritually.

God turns out to be Jesus! Christ sets up His millennial kingdom where Jew and Gentile are equally received and welcomed.

And many peoples will come and say, "Come, let us go up to the mountain of the Lord, to the house of the God of Jacob; that He may teach us concerning His ways, and that we may walk in His paths." For the law will go forth from Zion, and the word of the Lord from Jerusalem. And He will judge between the nations, and will render decisions for many peoples; and they will hammer their swords into plowshares, and their spears into pruning hooks. Nation will not lift up sword against nation, and never again will they learn war. (Isaiah 2:3–4)

The holocausts of this world will at last have ended!

WHERE WAS THE CHURCH?

Today many Jews are atheists because of the Holocaust. If there were a God, they reason, He could not have stood by without stopping the brutal injustice. Unfortunately, the church did not, for the most part, come to the aid of those who were ostracized or sent to the death camps. In fact, some joined in the persecutions.

Some justified their actions, contending that the Jews suffered because they called for Christ's blood after they rejected Him as the Messiah. The Jews did crucify Christ, but so did the Romans, and so did we. In the final analysis, Christ died voluntarily to give Himself up for us all. "For this reason the Father loves Me, because I lay down My life that I may take it again. No one has taken it away from Me, but I lay it down on My own initiative. I have authority to lay it down, and I have authority to take it up again" (John 10:17–18).

We should not think that the Jews had to suffer in the Holocaust because a past generation rejected Christ. Though the Jews squandered their high calling, so have the Gentiles. At the end of the day, we are all sinners in need of a Savior who "gave Himself for us" that we might be redeemed. The Jews were judged in the Holocaust, but so was Nazi Germany, which exalted a man in the place of God, and so was the church that gave the world the Reformation, then sank into the abyss of human aggrandizement.

The church simply failed to be the church.

In a letter sent to Right to Life supporters, there is a story that I reproduce here in summary form. In a small church on the East Coast a pastor delivered a sermon on abortion, and after the service a German man who had lived in Nazi Germany told of his experience:

> I lived in Germany during the Nazi Holocaust. I considered myself a Christian. We heard stories of what was happening to the

Jews, but we tried to distance ourselves from it, because, what could anyone do to stop it?

A railroad track ran behind our small church and each Sunday morning we could hear the whistle in the distance and then the wheels coming over the tracks. We became disturbed when we heard the cries coming from the train as it passed by. We realized that it was carrying Jews like cattle in the cars!

Week after week the whistle would blow. We dreaded to hear the sound of those wheels because we knew that we would hear the cries of the Jews en route to a death camp. Their screams tormented us.

We knew the time the train was coming and when we heard the whistle blow we began singing hymns. By the time the train came past our church we were singing at the top of our voices. If we heard the screams, we sang more loudly and soon we heard them no more.

Years have passed and no one talks about it anymore. But I still hear that train whistle in my sleep. God forgive me; forgive all of us who called ourselves Christians yet did nothing to intervene.

That story, which speaks so pointedly to the weakness of the church in Germany, speaks also to us: Do we hear the train here in America—the cries of the pre-born children in our abortion clinics, the abused child across the street, or the minorities who are daily discriminated against in the normal course of their existence? Or does our busy service for Christ drown out these muffled cries?

Unfortunately, only a few German Christians saw the Jews as their brothers and sisters; only a few saw them as Christ; only a few stood against the devils of hell that were unleashed by a satanic leader. A delegate to the 1950 Synod of the Evangelical Church in Germany declared, "In every train which carried Jews to their death-camps in the East, at least one Christian should have been a voluntary passenger."[17] Those who preserved their lives lost their honor. And in the end God used persecution to force His people to clarify their mission. There were reasons why the church was paralyzed, unable to find the strength to act.

The conflict was not so much between the church and Hitler as it was within the church itself. The question the church had to answer was, What does it mean for the church to be a church?

We now turn our attention to this struggle in which God proved that He would not allow His Son to be worshiped by those who would wrap His cross in a swastika.

CHAPTER FIVE

THE CHURCH IS DECEIVED

With a thicket of swastika flags surrounding the altar of the Magdeburg Cathedral, the dean, Dr. Martin, declared in 1933, "Whoever reviles this symbol of ours is reviling our Germany . . . the swastika flags around the altar radiate hope; hope that that day is at last about to dawn."[1]

Adoration for Hitler poured forth from pulpits of Germany. Pastor Siegfried Leffler proclaimed, "In the pitch-black night of church history, Hitler became, as it were, the wonderful transparency for our time, the window of our age, through which light fell on the history of Christianity. Through him we were able to see the Savior in the history of the Germans."[2]

On August 30, 1933, Pastor Julius Leutherser gushed, "Christ has come to us through Hitler . . . through his honesty, his faith and his idealism, the Redeemer found us. . . . We know today the Savior has come . . . we have only one task, be German, not Christian."[3] Clearly, even at this early point in the struggle, the swastika meant more to some pastors than did the Cross.

And so it was that the land that gave us Luther and Bach now gave the world Hitler and Wagner. The church that was called by God to stand against the evils of the Nazi regime came to embrace it. Swastikas, with the cross of Christ sometimes neatly woven in the center, adorned the churches. The broken cross of the political savior and the cross of the spiritual Savior would unite to lead Germany out of its abyss to the glorious heights of self-respect and unify the German-speaking areas of Europe. The Fatherland had been resurrected; the Germans could smile again.

Today pictures of this "holy union" startle us, but in Hitler's day being a good Christian involved being a good German nationalist. God and country were practically one and the same.

When the churchmen awoke from their spiritual and political slumbers, they discovered too late that they had been deceived. Early on only a few understood that Hitler was to be repudiated rather than revered, but their voices were drowned with the shouts of victory and celebration.

HATRED FOR THE JEWS, I'M SORRY TO SAY, ALSO FLOURISHED WITHIN THE CHURCHES.

We who have the advantage of a historical perspective are quick to judge; but if we had lived through those times, we too might have been duped by the nationalism of the day. If we were hungry with our economy in shambles and our country torn by political strife, we might be willing to believe anyone who had a plan to lead us out of our cultural swamp. We've already learned that the Weimar Republic was paralyzed politically, unable to do what needed to be done. Hitler had a plan and that was enough.

Germany, we have learned, was unified in its anger toward its enemies, whether real or imagined. The humiliating Treaty of Versailles, the Communists, and the liberal elite who believed in democracy—all of these were seen as threats to Germany's recovery. Even for those who called themselves Christians a strong Germany was more highly valued than a strong gospel witness, unless the gospel, as was often the case, was reinterpreted to be a plea for loyalty to the German cause.

Hatred for the Jews, I'm sorry to say, also flourished within the churches. Many Germans had read the works of Chamberlain and

A Nazi altar.

popular documents that pictured the Jews as traitors. And although the Jews constituted a small percentage of the population, they were seen as villains, responsible for the defeat of Germany in World War I. Although it was grudgingly acknowledged that Jesus was a Jew, it was also asserted that "occasionally a flower did grow in a dung heap." When Hitler called for a one-day boycott of Jewish businesses on April 1, 1933, many Christians supported him.

The churches were so enamored with Hitler's successes that they did not pause to ask in whose name these benefits had come to them. They spoke of the political resurgence as a revival, a time of renewal and spiritual strength. The churches derived strength from the improved economy and giddy optimism about a new day for Germany. Many of the wiser church members were not deceived, but the majority did not ask many questions. For now, what was good for Germany was good for the church.

Germany was about one-third Catholic and two-thirds Protestant. To its credit, the Catholic church stood against Hitler with a greater solidarity than the Protestants. Hitler knew that the Catholic church had an organizational network in many countries, so he preferred to maintain goodwill with the Vatican for as long as possible. In fact, a concordat was signed with the Vatican that guaranteed freedom of religion in exchange for political support. Unfortunately, when Hitler began to break his promises, the church leaders were confused. They had declared their loyalty to him; then they were forced to be disloyal. In the end they suffered essentially the same fate as the Protestants.

Many churchmen were duped. Father Falkan, a Catholic parish priest, said, "I must admit that I was glad to see the Nazis come to power, because at that time I felt that Hitler as a Catholic was a God-fearing individual who could battle communism for the Church . . . the anti-Semitism of the Nazis, as well as their anti-Marxism, appealed to the church."[4]

Hitler spoke of both Protestants and Catholics with contempt, convinced that all Christians would betray their God when they were forced to choose between the swastika and the Cross: "Do you really believe the masses will be Christian again? Nonsense! Never again. That tale is finished. No one will listen to it again. But we can hasten matters. The parsons will dig their own graves. They will betray their God to us. They will betray anything for the sake of their miserable jobs and incomes."[5]

Within a few weeks of taking power, on April 1, 1933, the Nazis organized anti-Jewish boycotts. The poster reads "The Jews have till 10 A.M. on Saturday to reflect. Then the struggle commences. The Jews of the world want to destroy Germany. German people—resist! Don't buy from Jews!"

"They will betray their God to us." Unfortunately, many pastors did just that. Several weaknesses of the church made such a temptation difficult to resist. In the dark night of persecution, they betrayed their God. In the end both Catholics and Protestants found themselves powerless to stop the Nazi steamroller. And yet, though the opposition from the church was weak, it was the only organized opposition Hitler had. Neither the universities nor the schools challenged him; and only part of the church had the courage to do so.

CHARACTERISTICS OF THE CHURCH

That Hitler deceived the church is clear enough. But we also must remember that the churches of Germany had already sold out to the popular themes of German culture long before Hitler rose to power. They were prepared to be deceived; some would say, wanted to be deceived. The deceptions did not happen all at once but were a part of a long history. The condition of the church prior to Hitler, says one historian, was just as much to blame as Hitler's opposition to the church.

NATIONALISM

Keep in mind that the church in Germany had a long history of being thoroughly nationalistic. During the Prussian dominance, the king was the head of the church. The clergy were servile to the political head of state. With such strong ties to the German monarchies, it is easy to see why the church fell into the snare of embracing the political agenda of the day.

I have stood in the Kaiser Wilhelm Memorial Church in Berlin (now a monument to the horrors of World War II) and have marveled at the reliefs of Christ and the Kaiser as if together they were the saviors of the German nation. Prussian military victories are depicted as victories for Christ and the Christian religion.

It should come as no surprise that Protestant leaders called for a synthesis of *Volkstum* (German national identity) and Christianity. Since the Protestant churches all belonged to more than twenty independent districts, the goal was that these regional churches be replaced by a *Reich's* church, that is, a centralized national church. Some leaders wanted to revise the church's creeds to bring them in line with national socialism. These became known as "German Christians" (with the emphasis on the word *German*). Thus when Hitler came to power, the large majority of these leaders welcomed him with enthusiasm. A strong Germany, they thought, meant a strong church.

The church found it almost impossible to stand against German culture; it stood transfixed, seemingly unable to challenge the assumptions of German nationalism and condemn it when necessary. Nationalism was so rife that during the Kaiser era, the Kaiser was seen as ruling by "divine right" as God's representative for the Christian nation. Soldiers who died in World War I were honored as martyrs for Christ.

The church joined in the general opposition to the democracy of the Weimar Republic and the liberties of individual conscience. Democracy was a weak form of government that paid too much attention to individual human rights. If the state was to be strong, individual freedoms had to be set aside for the greater good of a united, economically stable, and strong nation. Christians stood for the greatness of Germany, for its military might and prominence. They longed for a return to the good old days when a monarch ruled, order was restored, and victories were plentiful.

A man who lived in Nazi Germany told me that some Catholic priests threatened to withhold the sacraments from those parishioners who favored the Weimar Republic. Dedication services for Hitler's storm troopers were held in Protestant and Catholic churches; they were the heroes who were committed to a new Germany. They were fighting for the Fatherland, the advancement of a nation that deserved to put its humiliation behind it and become proud once more.

In a mood of worshipful euphoria, Professor Adam, a theologian of Tübingen, hailed Hitler as the one who had opened the eyes of the German people, united them, and freed them:

> Now he stands before us; he whom the voices of our poets and sages have summoned, the liberator of the German genius. He had removed the blindfold from our eyes, and through all political, economic and social and confessional covers has enabled us to see and love again the one essential thing—our unity of blood, our German self, the homo germanus.[6]

So it was that professors chimed in with the common man to sing Hitler's praises. The church was carried along by his growing popularity, a giddy hilarity that previously seemed so rare among sober-minded Germans. Large crowds flocked to Hitler's birthplace. Worshipers even journeyed by bus to honor the birthplace of his mother in Spittal. They descended on the farmhouse where Hitler spent his summers as a boy. John Toland writes, "They climbed on the roof to take pictures, found their way into the courtyard to wash at the wooden trough as if it contained holy water and chipped pieces from the large stones supporting the barn."[7] They painted swastikas on the cows and paraded around singing Hitler songs.

Those church members who were perceptive enough to realize that such idolatry would invite the judgment of God found it difficult to stand against the torrent of public adoration. In general, those who doubted kept their doubts to themselves.

LIBERALISM

The church, for the most part, had abandoned the historic Christian faith and had opted for theological liberalism; that is, they read the Bible trying to separate the true from the false, denying the uniqueness of Christ. Without a clear message of repentance and faith in Christ alone as the Son of God, the churches substituted the proud banner of a Christianized nationalism for the meekness and humility of Christ.

Martin Luther, though often quoted, was nevertheless not remembered as the man who preached a divine Christ who could reconcile totally depraved sinners to an infinitely holy God. The cross of Luther's Christ did not comfortably blend in with the swastika. In the presence of the Cross that Luther had proclaimed, men were humbled; the cross that so neatly fit within the swastika ignited pride.

Since all German infants were baptized into the church, little was said about the need for individual, adult conversion to Christ. The fact that one's name was on a church roll was proof enough that one was a Christian. All that was expected of good Christians was to help Germany become great.

Of course, there were some exceptions, as we shall see in subsequent chapters. There were genuine Christians sprinkled among the masses; there were a few who maintained that there was a vast difference between the Cross and the swastika. But for the most part, the church was caught up in the spirit of the age; it saw its role as helping erase the shame of the past and bringing about a better future. It rejoiced in a reversal of unemployment, in the improvement of the

A Nazi baptism.

standard of living, and the self-conscious dignity that revived a beleaguered nation.

Let evangelicals not think that there was always a neat division between the true Christians who were not deceived by Hitler and the nationalists who were. When Oswald J. Smith of the People's Church in Toronto (a missionary statesman and a man with impeccable evangelical credentials) visited Germany in 1936, he came back impressed by what Hitler had done for the country.

Smith's report was based on what he heard not from the liberal Christians but from those who were evangelical. Note also that Smith wrote in 1936, long after Hitler's party purges—when the persecution of the Jews had already begun. Germany, Smith said, "had awakened." Here is his report:

> What, you ask, is the real attitude of the German people toward Hitler? There is but one answer. They love him. Yes, from the highest to the lowest, children and parents, old and young alike—they love their

new leader. Their confidence in him cannot be shaken. They trust him to a man.

"What about your elections?" I asked. "You have no choice. It is Hitler or no one. There is no opponent." "We don't want another party," they replied with indignation. "We have had enough of parties. We want a true leader, a man who loves us, and works for our good. We are satisfied with Hitler." And that feeling exists everywhere. Every true Christian is for Hitler. I know for it was from the Christians I got most of my information, and right or wrong they endorse Adolf Hitler.[8]

Most interesting are Smith's comments about the treatment of the Jews. He was "sorry that the good Jews have had to suffer with the bad. But who can differentiate in an hour of mob rule and violence? Even Hitler could not restrain his followers."

Smith even believed that an evangelical awakening was coming to Germany, with the gospel of Christ preached in the churches. The Christian leaders assured him that as long as the gospel was preached, "Germany was safe."

Christians, whether liberal or conservative, should have known, however, that Germany was not "safe." As we shall see in the next chapter, the persecution of the church was heating up. The Lutherans were already divided on the question of whether the pastors should sign the Aryan clause, a statement that would forbid a person of Jewish blood to occupy a pulpit in Germany.

Christians of all kinds were deceived by Hitler, at least initially. The liberals, however, who were "tossed to and fro by every wind of doctrine" found themselves particularly vulnerable to the vortex of the Nazi whirlwind. Even when Hitler's agenda finally became clear, they were not willing to suffer for a gospel that they had long since abandoned. They were more interested in the miracles of a revived Germany than in the miracles on the pages of the New Testament. Salvation in this world was more important than salvation in an unseen life to come.

THE TWO SPHERES

We have been introduced to the doctrine of the "two spheres," which, popularly interpreted, means that Christ is Lord of the church, but the Kaiser (or the Führer) is, in a manner of speaking, lord over the political sphere. Allegiance to the political sphere was a high and honorable duty just as was allegiance to God. And allegiance to God was best demonstrated by allegiance to the state.

Thus the private values of honesty, sobriety, and compassion were not translated into public values. War was glorified; and the good of the state was exalted above that of the individual. And with the fervent belief that obedience to the state would produce a new society, Germans were willing to do whatever their Führer demanded. Their duty to God was spiritual; their duty to the state was political.

German children were taught prompt, explicit obedience to parents, teachers, and military commanders. Respect for *Ordnung* (order) was taught by ritual and threat of punishment. Everyone was to keep pace with the nation and its highest good. Romans 13:1–2 was often quoted: "Let every person be in subjection to the governing authorities. For there is no authority except from God, and those which exist are established by God. Therefore he who resists authority has opposed the ordinance of God; and they who have opposed will receive condemnation upon themselves."

WE MUST HAVE A MORE COMPLETE PICTURE OF WHAT IT MEANS FOR THE CHURCH TO ACTUALLY BE THE CHURCH IN SOCIETY.

Within the Lutheran church there was a strong pietistic movement that advocated a return to biblical piety, the worship of God within the heart. For the most part these people were opposed to biblical scholarship (especially of the liberal kind) and withdrew from the intellectual theological debates within Germany. They witnessed to the saving grace of Christ but believed that the church's mission was only to preach Christ.

Pietism, with its emphasis on personal devotion to Christ, was used to inject spiritual life into the mainstream Lutheran church. But by maintaining intense loyalty to the political authorities and insisting on obedience to the state even if it was contrary to one's personal convictions, pietism had scant influence in stemming the Nazi tide. A form of pietism is still popular among those in America today who believe that we should retreat from our cultural battles in favor of simply "preaching the gospel" and staying out of politics. What they forget is that as the state encroaches on our liberties, our spiritual sphere will continue to shrink until our very freedoms are taken away. No one will be able to run and hide.

James Dobson, in a letter sent to his supporters, challenged his readers with a series of questions: At what point will we be willing to defend what we believe? Will parents object if their children are routinely indoctrinated in homosexual ideology or occultism in the public schools? Will we object if the state tells pastors what they can or cannot say from the pulpit? (In Sweden an evangelical pastor who preached on Sodom and Gomorrah was convicted of "verbal violence" against homosexuals and sentenced to a four-week prison term.) Will we object if the state assumes ownership of our children and tells us how to rear them, or else lose custody? Will we object if every church has to hire a homosexual to satisfy a quota obligation?[9]

Whether in Nazi Germany or America today, believers cannot choose to remain silent under the guise of preaching the gospel. Sharing the gospel is, of course, our primary responsibility since it is only the cross of Christ that can transform the human heart. But once we have received the gift of salvation through Christ, we must live out the implications of the Cross in every area of our lives. In fact, our very right to preach the gospel will be in jeopardy if we are not prepared to submit to the lordship of Christ in all spheres.

Those who dutifully accepted the excesses of the Nazi regime, but simply continued to study the Bible to maintain a warm heart, are to be commended for getting it half right. Certainly they were much more effective than those who ceased to study their Bibles and enthusiastically endorsed the regime. But as we shall see in a future chapter, we must have a more complete picture of what it means for the church to actually be the church in society.

Hitler would soon try to force the church to adopt what he called "positive Christianity" that was more radical than even the most nationalistic churches had anticipated. His plan, as it would later be unveiled, called for the obliteration of the church. In the end, he wanted to transform the church so thoroughly that every vestige of Christianity would be smashed. There was not enough room in the church for both the Cross and the swastika. As he himself mused, "One god must dominate another." Given the weaknesses of the church, his goal appeared to be within reach, though it would not be as easy as he thought.

HITLER CAPTURES A NATION

Hitler began by demanding an inch, then a yard, and finally a whole mile. He transformed society and in so doing he also transformed the church. He could not be at rest until his broken cross replaced the cross of Christ. Hitler's strategy to seduce the German people consisted of three stages.

THE LIES OF THE STATE

Hitler believed in lies. He said that "the magnitude of a lie always contains a certain factor of credibility since the great masses of people . . . more easily fall victim to a big lie than to a little one." He shaped the culture and religion of Germany with lies that were soon reflected in laws.

After he was sworn in as chancellor, he paid tribute to Christianity as "an essential element for safeguarding the soul of the German people" and promised to respect the rights of the churches. He declared his ambition to have "a peaceful accord between Church and state."[10] He also expressed intentions to improve his relationship with Pope Pius XII.

He was willing to give the churches freedom, he said, "as long as they did not do anything subversive to the state." Of course, behind that promise lay his own definition of what might be subversive. But his guarded promise, as well as a concordat with the Vatican that guaranteed freedom to the Catholic church, was welcomed.

Article 24 of the party platform demanded "liberty for all religious denominations in the State so far as they are not a danger . . . to the moral feelings of the German race." Hitler spoke approvingly of his "positive Christianity," which would contribute to the German struggle. He won some goodwill by appearing to be conciliatory; the churches liked his use of the word "freedom." Apparently he hoped that the people would feel good about him in the beginning, even if they didn't feel so good about him later on.

Privately, however, Hitler revealed his true intentions. Herman Rauschning records that shortly after his ascent to power Hitler remarked that there was no future for either Catholic or Protestant denominations. Making peace with the church, he said, "won't stop me from stamping out Christianity in Germany, root and branch. One is either a Christian or a German. You can't be both."[11]

On March 21, 1933, Hitler arranged an impressive spectacle for the opening of the new session of the Reichstag in the Garrison Church in Potsdam. With pomp and ceremony he sought to assure the nation that he could follow a conservative path and seek harmony with the churches. Two days later, the Reichstag passed the so-called "Enabling Law" whereby the power of the Reichstag was reduced to a sounding board for the party. The necessary majority to pass the bill was secured by the arrest of some Parliament members and the threatening of others. By July Hitler proclaimed the Nazis as the only party in Germany.

But in those early days, the words "freedom" and "peace" were found in all of his speeches. That gave the masses the reassurance that though they might have some misgivings, once they understood him better, they would know that he was on their side.

Next, Hitler, a master of deceit, looked for a pretext, an excuse for exercising greater control. Just as the Reichstag fire was an excuse for suspending personal liberties, so he created other opportunities that gave him the privilege of bypassing conventional means of justice.

As a prelude to an attempted takeover of the church, Hitler removed some of his opposition by falsely accusing churchmen of treason, theft, or sexual malpractices. Goebbels, the propaganda minister, insisted that those trials be published in detail in newspapers, thus parading lurid details about known ministers, priests, and nuns. Priests who warned parents against letting their children become a part of the Hitler Youth were subject to blackmail. Thus Hitler silenced the mouths of those who would dare oppose him. Catholic priests, nuns, and church leaders were arrested on trumped-up charges, and religious publications were suppressed.

Hitler always said that the best way to conquer your enemies is to divide them. He encouraged a movement simply called "God Believers," designed to persuade individuals to withdraw from the churches. The sales pitch was that there was an alternative to the church; whatever it accomplished could be done elsewhere and in other ways. The state could have a ceremony to dedicate infants; the state could have its own holidays without the need to celebrate the Christian ones.

Marriages, for those who wished, could also be performed by the state. The blessing of Mother Earth and Father Sky were frequently invoked upon the couple in order that their destiny might be fulfilled. When the state christened an infant, the father carried the child on a shield wrapped with a blanket of undyed wool, embroidered with swastikas. The child was, in effect, dedicated to the German state and its name written in the register.

In 1935 prayers ceased to be obligatory in schools; religious instruction was not yet exactly prohibited, but it was limited to those who had been licensed by the state. Thus the dogmas of Nazism were substituted for the doctrines of the Bible. The schools taught their subjects through the eyes of the regime.

Since Germans had for centuries celebrated Christmas and Easter, Hitler had to reinterpret their meaning. Christmas was turned into a totally pagan festival; in fact, at least for the SS troops, its date was changed to December 21, the date for winter solstice. Carols and Nativity plays were banned from the schools in 1938, and even the name Christmas was changed to "Yuletide." Crucifixes were eliminated from classrooms, and Easter was turned into a holiday that heralded the arrival of spring.

You will recognize the same changes taking place in America today, thanks to our social libertarians, who are bent on scrubbing the state of even the remnants of Christianity. What Hitler achieved through his edicts can also be achieved through the courts of our land. Though crime is out of control, illegitimacy is skyrocketing, and drugs are destroying our youth, the ACLU has dedicated itself to stamping out all "state sponsored" observance of religious holidays. No carols in schools; no Nativity scenes in town halls; no crosses on public property.

Not unlike some of our own liberated social planners, Hitler preached that the children belonged to the Reich. To parents, Hitler calmly said, "Your child belongs to us already . . . what are you? You will pass on. Your descendants, however, now stand in the new camp. In a short time they will know nothing else but this new community." And in another speech he said, "This new Reich will give its youth to no one, but will itself take youth and give to youth its own education and its own upbringing."[12]

The Hitler Youth competed with the educational system of the state. Private schools were abolished, and by 1938 all education was unified under the Nazi ideology. Textbooks were rewritten to reflect the view of racial fitness, the rationale for military expansion, and an emphasis on German history and culture. Those who did not fall in line with the Nazi agenda (read "politically correct") were reprimanded, expelled, or executed. If teachers wanted to keep their jobs, they had to take an oath of loyalty to Hitler.

Book burning was common. While visiting Berlin, I stood in the square opposite Berlin University (now called Humbolt University) where, on the evening of May 10, 1933, a torchlight parade for thousands of students was held to burn an estimated twenty thousand books. Many of these were written by famous Germans and other authors of worldwide distinction, such as H. G. Wells and Jewish physicist Albert Einstein. Goebbels, Hitler's propaganda minister, addressed the students, "The soul of the German people can again express itself. These flames not only illuminate the final end of an old era; they also light up the new."[13]

Initially there was significant opposition to Hitler's agenda. But few spoke against it because of fear of reprisals. Also, the people longed to believe the myth that after Hitler consolidated his power, he would relax and allow more freedoms. Others accepted these new ideas as a kind of exchange for the economic and political benefits that they now had. Too late did they realize that these were only the initial stages of a complete Nazi takeover.

The nation that had been seduced by propaganda was then headed for persecution. The lies became laws.

THE LAWS OF THE STATE

Laws always reflect a nation's priorities, agenda, and values. In Nazi Germany laws were no longer seen as resting on a theistic, much less a Christian, view of the world; indeed not even natural law was recognized. When Hitler got the Reichstag to give him the power to make the laws, the laws he made were arbitrary, drafted to fulfill the goals of the state. The Nazis proclaimed, "Hitler is the law!" As Göring put it, "The law and the will of the Führer are one."[14] *Right and wrong was whatever Hitler said it was.*

The Nuremberg laws of September 15, 1935, deprived Jews of German citizenship, confining them to the status of "subjects." They forbade marriage between Jews and Aryans and sexual relationships between them. This was the basis for thirteen specific laws against the Jews that would outlaw them completely. Many of them were deprived of their livelihood and faced starvation. In many towns they were forbidden to purchase food or do business.

There were also laws against treason. Treason was defined as anything that was contrary to the will and the purposes of the Reich. Criticism was treason; freedom of the press was treason; a failure to further the agenda of the Reich was treason. Once again, treason was whatever Hitler said it was.

In 1936, the People's Court was established to try acts of treason. Five judges were appointed to each court, three of whom were always appointed by Hitler or one of his associates "because of their special knowledge in the defense against subversive activities or because they are more intimately connected with the political trends of the nation." The proceedings were secret, the punishment severe. Crimson red posters announced the names of those who died under the ax of the executioner.

The experience of Nazi Germany reminds us that whoever controls a nation's laws controls a nation's agenda and values. Rausas Rushdoony put it well: "Behind every system of law there is a god. To find the god in any system, locate the source of law in that system." Whether the source of law is a dictator, the courts, or an individual, that person(s) is the god of that system. He adds, "When you choose your authority, you choose your god, and where you look for your law, there is your god."15

With his place as dictator assured, Hitler could make whatever laws he wished and mock his seemingly powerless opposition. He had always regarded Protestants with contempt, saying of them, "You can do anything you want with them. . . . They will submit . . . they are insignificant little people, submissive as dogs, and they sweat with embarrassment when you talk to them."16 He knew that resistance to his agenda came only from a small minority of Protestant leaders.

Thankfully, not all Protestants were "as submissive as dogs." In the next chapters of this book we shall meet some of those who stood up to Hitler at great personal cost. But there were too few, too late.

THE LORD OF THE STATE

Hitler began with *lies;* they were reflected in his *laws,* and finally he emerged as *lord.* He had achieved the near absolute control his demented heart desired.

If we ask why Hitler saw Christianity (even the nationalized German variety) as a threat, the answer was given in a television interview I saw with a man who was a contemporary of the Führer. In response to the question as to why Hitler felt such a need to destroy Christianity, the man said simply, "In any conflict among Gods, one must dominate another."

"SHOW ME YOUR LAWS AND I WILL SHOW YOU YOUR GOD!"

Before we turn to look at the struggle that took place within the church, we must understand what Hitler's ultimate goal was for the National Reich Church that he attempted to organize. I am reproducing part of a thirty-point program drawn up by Hitler's good friend Alfred Rosenberg, who blasphemed Christ and insisted that the church replace Christianity with the paganism of the Nazi movement. Here are some of the chilling articles of the program:

1. The National Reich Church of Germany categorically claims the exclusive right and the exclusive power to control all churches within the borders of the Reich; it declares these to be national churches of the German Reich.

   . . . .

13. The National Church demands immediate cessation of the publishing and dissemination of the Bible in Germany.

14. The National Church declares that to it, and therefore to the German nation, it has been decided that the Führer's *Mein Kampf* is the greatest of all documents. It . . . not only contains the greatest but it embodies the purest and truest ethics for the present and future life of our nation.

    . . . .

18. The National Church will clear away from its altars all crucifixes, Bibles, and pictures of saints.

19. On the altars there must be nothing but *Mein Kampf* [to the German nation and therefore to God the most sacred book] and to the left of the altar a sword.

. . . .

30. On the day of its foundation, the Christian Cross must be removed from all churches, cathedrals and chapels . . . and it must be superseded by the only unconquerable symbol, the swastika.[17]

Please note that it was not enough that the swastika be alongside the cross; it had to completely replace it. The Bible could not be laid alongside of *Mein Kampf,* but the Nazi bible had to be on the altar by itself. In short, the God of heaven had to be removed to make way for the god of national socialism.

THE POWER OF A NATION'S LAWS

By now it should be clear that the moral landscape of a country is largely determined by its laws. When Hitler made the laws, Germany was molded into his own image. As Rushdoony in effect said, "Show me your laws and I will show you your God!"

After Hitler was defeated, war crimes trials were held in Nuremberg to judge the guilt of Hitler's henchmen. But a dispute arose as to what laws should be used to try the accused. After all, Hitler's cronies argued, quite plausibly, that they had not broken any laws; their actions were carried out with the protection of their own legal system. They could not be accused of murder because personhood had been redefined to exclude Jews and other undesirables. These men were simply following the laws handed down by the courts of their day. As Eichmann protested before his execution, "I was simply following the laws of war and my flag."

Here in America, a group of protesters who picketed an abortion clinic were charged with slander for calling abortionists murderers. The abortionists argued, just as Hitler's emissaries had done, that they could not be murderers because they were not breaking any laws. The experience of Nuremberg and the silent holocaust in our abortion clinics bear eloquent witness to the fact that when a state is accountable to no one except itself, it assumes that whatever is legal is moral. The law is simply whatever the courts say it is.

The dispute at Nuremberg was resolved when Robert H. Jackson, chief counsel for the United States, was forced to appeal to permanent values, to standards that transcended that of any particular society. He argued that there was a "law above the law" that stood in judgment on the arbitrary opinions of men. However, I firmly believe that apart from divine revelation, no such laws can be derived from nature or experience.[18]

As we in America move toward arbitrary sociological laws, the state will expand its powers and the church will be expected either to go along with the changes or face the consequences.

Antichrist, like Hitler, will also transform his world by changing the laws. Daniel 7:25 says that he will "make alterations in times and in law." Like Hitler he will begin with lies, then make laws, and finally be worshiped as lord. His control will be expanded both in numbers and invading the details of ordinary living. He will be another Hitler, more powerful, more believable, more blasphemous, more cruel.

Hitler believed deeply that propaganda had to precede the state's transformation. Here in America we can see how the media can shape the values of a culture and help bring about a society that is at war with the values of the past. Whether it is abortion, special homosexual rights, or an agenda of "political correctness" that restricts free speech, the attitudes of a nation can change if enough people say the same thing often enough. Lies often end up as laws.

We have sketched the big picture. Now let's look at these events from within the church. Let's try to understand the struggle, listen to the debates, and learn from those who can instruct us. And let us imagine what we would do if we had lived during those perilous times.

CHAPTER SIX

THE CHURCH IS DIVIDED

C onfess! Confess! Confess!"
The words reverberated in the sanctuary
of the Trinity Lutheran Church in Berlin. A
young theologian was pleading with the congregation to awaken to
its responsibility at an hour when its witness and strength were
most sorely needed. He insisted that if the church stood upon
Christ as the Rock then,

> the church will not be taken from us. . . . Come you who have been
> left alone, you who have lost the church, let us return to Holy Writ,
> let us go forth and seek the church together. . . . For the times, which
> are times of collapse to the human understanding may well be for
> her a great time of building. . . . Church, remain a church . . . con-
> fess! confess! confess![1]

The date was July 23, 1933. The young theologian was Dietrich
Bonhoeffer. In January of the same year, Hitler had been installed as
chancellor of Germany. The very next day, this young man, who was
not duped by the Führer's intentions, gave a radio address in which
he warned that when a people idolize a leader "the image of the leader will gradually become the image of the 'misleader.' Thus the leader
makes an idol of himself and mocks God." Before these last sentences

were broadcast, Bonhoeffer's microphone was mysteriously switched off.

Bonhoeffer kept reminding anyone who would listen that the church has only one altar before which it must kneel, and that is the altar of the Almighty. The pride of the church, he said, must be rebuked by the humiliation of the Cross. "God's victory means our defeat, it means our humiliation; it means God's mocking anger at all human arrogance, being puffed up, trying to be important in our own right. It means the Cross above the world. . . . The cross of Christ, that means the bitter scorn of God for all human heights, bitter suffering of God in all human depths, the rule of God over the whole world . . . with Gideon we kneel before the altar and say, 'Lord on the Cross, be thou alone our Lord. Amen.'"[2]

The crisis of which he spoke was only partly a conflict between Hitler and Christianity. It was primarily a struggle of the church against itself; it was the struggle of the false and the true, the swastika and the Cross. It was a struggle within a church that had voluntarily embraced the German nationalism of the day. Bonhoeffer insisted that only a Christ who was free of German national ideals and culture could rescue the church at this critical hour. The church must proclaim a Christ who stands above politics, above the sacred and the secular.

The "German Christians," whom we met in the last chapter, were committed to bringing the church in line with Nazism. They were in favor of disbanding the authority of individual districts to unite all Protestants into a Reich Church, that is, one all-encompassing, national church. Of course there was much opposition to the plan, but they believed that if done through free elections, the integrity of the church could be maintained.

Hitler surprised Protestants by insisting that his personal friend Ludwig Müller be elected Reich bishop. Obviously, there was immediate opposition to this intrusion of the state into the "spiritual sphere." The Lutherans were divided. Some supported a man named Dr. Bodelschwingh, a respected man of deep piety. The "German Christians," who were also known as "The Faith Movement," supported Hitler's candidate. After vigorous debate at a conference of regional delegates, on May 27, 1933 Bodelschwingh was elected by a majority. In his acceptance speech he promised that he would remain above the debates within his church and simply place himself at the disposal of the church for "service to the nation."

The next weeks showed that that kind Christian man was blind to the importance of the ideological currents that swirled within the Lutheran church. He didn't realize that it was impossible for him to stay "above the battle" in a church that had so willingly aligned itself with Nazism.

The "German Christians" opposed him with open hostility. They attacked him in the press and on radio, insisting that Müller would be better qualified to lead the church because of his close ties with Hitler. The Reich bishop, they said, should only be elected after a new constitution was ratified. Under pressure, Bodelschwingh was forced to resign. This triggered the resentment of those who were incensed at the heavy-handed tactics of the pro-Nazi forces. Fifty pastors signed a statement of protest.

Meanwhile the "German Christians" completed a new church constitution that was recognized by the Reichstag on July 14, 1933. Their slogan was "One State, One People, One Church." They endorsed Hitler's "positive Christianity," saying as did Hermann Gruner, "Hitler is the way of the Spirit and the will of God for the German people to enter the Church of Christ."[3] These Christians adorned their altars with Nazi flags and had their congregations join in the Nazi salute.

A week later, on July 23, a national election was scheduled, and Hitler went on the radio to back all the candidates throughout Germany supported by the "German Christians." In his speech he said that the state wanted to guarantee the independence of the church, but this could only happen if the church had leaders who were committed to "the freedom of this nation." Then he went on to give a direct endorsement to the "German Christians," commending them for their support of the National Socialist State. Thousands of people who for years had not darkened the door of a church voted and, to no one's surprise, Hitler's candidates won. All that was needed was for Ludwig Müller to be elected Reich bishop by the church representatives.

Bonhoeffer was deeply distressed. The next month, August of 1933, he sent a letter to his grandmother, predicting that there was a powerful movement toward a big, popular national church whose nature could not be reconciled with Christianity. He said that "we must be prepared to enter upon entirely new paths which we shall have to tread. The conflict is really Germanism or Christianity and the sooner the conflict comes out in the open the better. Nothing could be more dangerous than its concealment."[4]

The next month the conflict came out in the open.

THE BROWN SYNOD

On September 5 and 6, 1933, the old Prussian General Synod met in Berlin for a two-day session. Delegations of pastors and church leaders arrived wearing Nazi uniforms and giving the Nazi salute. The synod quickly took on the nature of a demonstration rather than a discussion session. They confirmed Ludwig Müller as their bishop and dismissed current general superintendents in order to replace them with those who were loyal to the National Socialist agenda. They adopted what is known as the Aryan Clause, which barred those who were of Jewish blood from the pulpits of Germany. All pastors would be required to sign this statement and give "unconditional support to the National Socialist State." When opposition was voiced, it was shouted down.

THE CHURCH IS THE PLACE WHERE THE CHRISTIAN JEW AND GENTILE "STAND TOGETHER UNDER GOD'S WORD"; ONLY SUCH SUBMISSION PROVES WHETHER THE CHURCH IS STILL THE CHURCH.

This synod, known as "the Brown Synod" (thanks to the Nazi SA uniforms worn by the delegates), did not insist that those who were presently pastors of Jewish blood resign, but only that new Jewish applicants would be ineligible for ministry. All pastors were then required to give proof that they were of Aryan ancestry.

The responsibility of taking minutes at this infamous meeting had fallen on the shoulders of none other than Martin Niemöller, a man whose name would become famous for his resistance to the Nazification of the church. He had been a naval lieutenant and submarine commander in World War I but was ordained in 1924 and became an influential pastor in a Berlin suburb. Initially he welcomed the Nazi party, believing it was the best hope for Germany. In fact, he sent

Hitler a telegram congratulating him on Germany's withdrawal from the League of Nations and thanking him for his "manly act and clear statement in defense of Germany's honor." The telegram ended with an expression of "loyal and prayerful support."

Having observed the Brown Synod firsthand, Niemöller knew that the time for active protest had arrived. He had become friends with Dietrich Bonhoeffer, and they met to discuss what could be done. Bonhoeffer had written a paper exposing the absurdity of barring someone from the church on biological grounds. The church, he said, is the place where the Christian Jew and Gentile "stand together under God's Word"; only such submission proves whether the church is still the church.

Other church leaders tried to put the best face on the Synod's decision, saying that there were perhaps only about eleven pastors in Prussia who would be affected by it; perhaps this concession to Nazism should be overlooked in the interest of the more important issue of "spreading the Gospel."

Bonhoeffer and Niemöller called for widespread resignations from the church. At the very time when the "German Christians" were celebrating their victory, God was at work. His hand of judgment was heavy upon the church, but He was also remembering mercy. He was giving His people an opportunity to declare themselves. Those who believed that the gospel should not be compromised had an opportunity to "confess Christ before men."

To quote the words of one observer, "God's judgments were the veil of His ever-present grace." His veiled grace would give the true believers the courage they needed.

THE PASTORS' EMERGENCY LEAGUE

On September 21, 1933, just two weeks after the Brown Synod, Niemöller and Bonhoeffer met with a group called "the Young Reformers" to form the Pastors' Emergency League. They pledged to fight the Aryan Clause and take a stand against the intrusion of Nazism in the church. We should keep in mind that they were not taking a stand against Nazism as a political force but only insisting that it not invade the spiritual sphere. A letter signed by both of them was sent to the pastors.[5] Specifically, the aims of the League were as follows:

1. To renew their allegiance to the Scriptures and the creed.

2. To resist those who attacked the Scriptures and the creed.
3. To give material and financial aid to those who suffered through repressive laws or violence.
4. To repudiate the Aryan Clause.

Almost immediately the letter garnered about two thousand signatures, and by the end of 1933 the numbers swelled to six thousand. The new bishops who had been elected on a pro-Hitler agenda were, of course, angry and silent.

THE SWASTIKA WAS, IN EFFECT, ADOPTED AS THE NEW CROSS IN THE VERY CATHEDRAL WHERE LUTHER HAD PREACHED THE CROSS OF CHRIST FOUR HUNDRED YEARS BEFORE!

When a questionnaire was sent to all the pastors, requiring that they give evidence of their personal ancestry, Niemöller refused to comply and urged others to follow his lead. He knew his action was disobedient to the state, but he took seriously the words of Scripture: "There is neither Jew nor Greek, there is neither slave nor free man, there is neither male nor female; for you are all one in Christ Jesus" (Galatians 3:28). He and Bonhoeffer believed that those who signed the Aryan Clause were separating themselves from the church of Christ.

The Pastors' Emergency League would soon have an opportunity to test its strength by making a formal protest. Six days after the letter was sent to the pastors, a National Synod was held to formally take the recommendation of the Prussian Synod and elect Ludwig Müller to the position of Reich bishop, thus unifying all Protestant denominations in one national organization. There was no opposition candidate.

Ironically, the synod was held in the Castle Church in Wittenberg, where Martin Luther had nailed his ninety-five theses. Ludwig Müller was unanimously elected as Reich bishop, and other "German

National Synod at Wittenberg, 1933.

Christians" were elected as regional bishops right beside the tomb where Luther was buried. Thus, in one of those ironies whose symbolism cannot be missed, *the swastika was, in effect, adopted as the new cross in the very cathedral where Luther had preached the cross of Christ four hundred years before!*

Niemöller and Bonhoeffer were present at the meeting in Wittenberg on September 27, 1933. They distributed leaflets to the delegates and nailed them to trees. "We will not cease to combat everything that is destructive to the very nature of the Church." As for the National Church's response to the leaflets, it was later reported that Wittenberg had been full of rumors and that "the enemy is making his presence felt."

When Ludwig Müller was elected, Bonhoeffer, who was standing at the back of the church, whispered to a friend, "You have just witnessed the death of the church in Germany!" Actually, the false church had already died, and although the true church was about to embark on a struggle for its existence, life would still emanate from it.

Bonhoeffer, who had committed himself to making the church what it should be, then faced an important decision: Should he continue the struggle against the Nazism from within Germany itself, or should he take the opportunity to go overseas? After reflection he made his decision.

BONHOEFFER LEAVES GERMANY

Bonhoeffer had been teaching at the University of Berlin and had grown disillusioned with the university's acceptance of the Nazi philosophy. Since he was rejected for the pastorate in Germany because of his theological views, he chose to accept the pastorate of two German-speaking churches in London. Though criticized by some who thought he was simply fleeing the battle, he insisted that he was only changing his strategy. From London he stirred up opposition to the German Reich Church. He attempted to rally international churches to take a stronger anti-Nazi stand and to support the Confessing Church.

At an international gathering of the World Alliance in Denmark, Bonhoeffer gave a stinging address in which he asked how the churches could justify their existence if they did not take measures to halt the steady march of Germany toward war. He demanded that the ecumenical council speak out "so that the world, though it gnash its teeth, will have to hear, so that the peoples will rejoice because the church of Christ in the name of Christ has taken the weapons from the hands of their sons, forbidden war, proclaimed the peace of Christ against the raging world."[6]

Here Bonhoeffer presented one of his strongest affirmations of pacifism, proclaiming that Christians may not use weapons against one another because they know that in so doing they are aiming those weapons at Christ Himself. In one memorable sentence he said, "Peace must be dared; it is a great venture."

Two years later Bonhoeffer would return to Germany and begin a seminary for those studying to lead the Confessing Church. Eventually, retreating from pacifism, he would join a conspiracy to assassinate Hitler.

THE "GERMAN CHRISTIANS"
REVEAL THEIR AGENDA

On November 13, 1933, the "German Christians" staged a massive rally in the Sports Palace in Berlin. The demonstration opened with a procession of Nazi flags. Then a choir sang "Now Thank We All Our God," and a chorus of trumpets blared out "A Mighty Fortress Is Our God." In opening remarks it was said that the "Faith Movement" had not yet achieved all of its goals and the "enemy had to be pursued until he fled in disarray."

Then Dr. Krause, a dignitary of the "German Christians," gave a sensational, if not blasphemous, speech to the twenty thousand people present. He pled for a second German "Reformation." Interrupted by thunderous applause, he declared that if the church was to find a home in Germany, the first step was

> the liberation from all that is un-German in liturgy and confession, liberation from the Old Testament with its Jewish recompense ethic, from all these stories about cattle-dealers and pimps. . . . Our provincial church will also have to see to it that all obviously distorted and superstitious reports should be expunged from the New Testament, and that the whole scapegoat and inferiority-type theology of the Rabbi Paul should be renounced in principle, for it has perpetuated a falsification of the Gospel.[7]

Another speaker complained that "the exaggerated display of the crucified Jesus is intolerable in the German Church."

Luther, needless to say, would have been scandalized by this "Second Reformation," with its repudiation of the Old Testament, the belittling of Christ, and the charge that Paul was to be discarded because he falsified the gospel. Most of all he would have called the church to repentance for casting down the cross of Christ by wedding it to a pagan political agenda. The church, he would have declared, had left Christ to follow Antichrist.

The meeting ignited a storm of controversy. Even some "German Christians" were offended. Krause had to resign his position, and many leaders began to back away from the radical Nazification of the church. But the damage had been done. The "German Christians" would from then on be associated with the radical anti-Jewish, anti-Christian, anti-Pauline doctrines exposed at the meeting. Even Hitler backed away from his support of the "German Christians," fearing that the growing split would only be harder to contain. He knew he needed the support of the church for his coming military adventures.

Niemöller could not remain silent. He protested to Reich Bishop Müller on behalf of the Emergency League, calling upon him to dismiss all the bishops who had not protested the blasphemous utterances. On the following Sunday, members of the league read a statement of protest to their congregations.

NIEMÖLLER MEETS HITLER

On January 4, 1934, Reich Bishop Müller issued what became known as the "Muzzling Order," a decree to restore order to the German Evangelical Church. Ministers were forbidden to include any matters of church controversy in their sermons. He said that the church service was "for the proclamation of the pure Gospel, and for this alone."

Pastors were faced with the question of what constituted "the pure Gospel." Could a pastor be faithful to his flock simply by preaching Christ and Him crucified? Or were there implications that must be lived out in the lives of Christians? What was the pastor's role in warning the flock and instructing his people about the dangers of another cross? Though the decree threatened expulsion, thousands of pastors defied Müller's order.

Hitler began to realize that it would be more difficult to subdue the church than he had originally thought. He said he learned that "one cannot break the Church over one's knee. It has to be left to rot like a gangrenous limb . . . but the healthy youth belongs to us." Eventually, he would, of course, "attempt to break the church over his knee," but for the time being he wanted to appear conciliatory.

So in an outward show of good faith on January 25, 1934, Hitler summoned the leaders of the churches to a personal conference in which Niemöller was included. Hitler had received word that a split might be developing within the church, and he wanted to prevent his own bishop from being discredited. So Niemöller and other members of the clergy walked past the SS guards to the Reich chancellery in Berlin and soon were ushered into Hitler's study. The Reich bishop, Ludwig Müller, stood behind the Führer.

Hitler began by reproaching his guests, treating them to a tirade about how he had been misunderstood. "Peace," he said, was all that he wanted, "peace between Church and state." He blamed them for obstructing him, for sabotaging his efforts to achieve that peace.

Niemöller was waiting for a chance to speak and, when he had the opportunity, explained that his only object was the welfare of the church, the state, and the German people. Hitler listened in silence and then said, "You confine yourself to the Church. I'll take care of the German people." The conversation then drifted to other themes.

When it was over, Hitler shook hands with the clergy, and Niemöller realized it would be his last opportunity to speak his mind. Carefully choosing his words he said, "You said that 'I will take care of the German people.' But we too, as Christians and churchmen, have a responsibility toward the German people. That responsibility was entrusted to us by God, and neither you nor anyone in this world has the power to take it from us."[8] Hitler turned away without a word.

That evening, eight Gestapo men ransacked Niemöller's rectory for incriminating material. A few days later a homemade bomb exploded in his hall. The police came to the scene even though no one had called them. The threats were easier for Niemöller to bear than some of the criticism he received from his colleagues for his strong words to Hitler.

In his biography entitled *Pastor Niemöller,* Dietmar Schmidt says that Niemöller "found himself the object of almost universal reproach" among his own supporters. They blamed him for the failure of the conference because of his words to Hitler. They predicted that instead of Müller's being dismissed from office, Hitler would actually strengthen his friend's hand. One pastor sought to ostracize Niemöller altogether, saying, "I see Pastor Niemöller is among us. I am not aware that we have anything further to discuss with him." Niemöller got up and left the building without a word.

Clearly the majority of the clergy had adopted an attitude of safety first. Various bishops began to defect from their commitment to a church free of political interference. Some signed on with the "German Christians," insisting that there could be compromise between the church and state. A few days later two thousand pastors resigned from the Pastors' Emergency League. They believed that Niemöller had gone too far in being disloyal to the growing tide of support for Hitler's political and economic achievements.

To be fair, we must point out that some of these pastors returned to side with Niemöller in later years. Dietmar Schmidt writes, "For the fact is that there were not always clear-cut 'fronts' in the religious battles of the 30's. The German Christians and their opponents never comprised a solid phalanx." Each man had to decide for himself where he stood, keeping an eye open for Hitler's next move. In all of these battles, says Schmidt, "personal ambition, timidity, indecision and opportunism were just as much in evidence as courage, consistency and Christian zeal."[9]

The day before Hitler's meeting with the pastors, he had appointed an old friend, Alfred Rosenberg, to the task of the spiritual training of the Nazi party. Rosenberg's aim, as we learned in the last chapter, was the creation of a German church in which there would be no place for the teaching of Christ. He claimed that "the eternal truths were not to be found in the Gospels . . . but in the Germanic ideals of character, and education in Germany must in the future be based on the 'fact' that the Germanic character, not Christianity was the source of virtue."[10] He wanted to replace the Bible with *Mein Kampf* or preferably his own book, *The Myth of the Twentieth Century,* which taught that the German people were the godhead that all should worship.

THE CHURCH HAD TO CHOOSE BETWEEN A CHRIST WHO WAS LORD OVER A SHRINKING "SPIRITUAL SPHERE" AND A CHRIST WHO WAS "LORD OVER ALL."

Thus 1933 ended and 1934 began with the German church in crisis. The initial optimism that the church might form a solid block of opposition to Hitler had faded. Worse, the battle had hardly begun. As time went on the church would endure even more tough choices. More battles would yet have to be won—or lost.

THE FORMATION OF THE CONFESSING CHURCH (1934)

Under the leadership of Bonhoeffer and Niemöller, the Pastors' Emergency League formed the nucleus of what was called the Confessing Church. Bonhoeffer had preached that the church should be the church and "Confess! Confess! Confess!" The time for public and sustained confessing had begun.

THE BARMEN CONFESSION

In May 1934, the Confessing Church met and adopted the Barmen Confession drafted by Swiss theologian Karl Barth. Although

Bonhoeffer was not present for the meeting, he had helped in preparation for the event through communication from London and visits to Europe. His courageous leadership helped pave the way for its acceptance.

In his book *The Church's Confession Under Hitler,* Arthur C. Cochrane writes that the Barmen Confession is "the most significant Church document that has appeared since the Reformation."[11] The church had to choose between a Christ who was Lord over a shrinking "spiritual sphere" and a Christ who was "Lord over all." Bonhoeffer had said that the "church should be the church." Barmen sought to answer the question of what the church should be.

Divisions within the church are, of course, necessary and sanctioned by Scripture. Paul wrote to the carnal Corinthians, "For there must also be factions among you, in order that those who are approved may have become evident among you" (1 Corinthians 11:19). When apostasy is rife, those who hold the truth must march under a different flag. Though they didn't want to divide the church, those who signed the Confession knew their document would do so.

The pastors who signed the declaration drew a line in the sand; they chose to reaffirm the mission of the church at a time when it was being redefined by the religious/political culture of the day. They gathered to resist unanimously the exaltation of the state above the church. No doubt they had many disagreements about other points in theology, but they did agree on the need for a church to be accountable only to the Christ of the Scriptures.

In response to criticism that they intended to split the church, the preamble of the Confession read, "The unity of the Evangelical Churches in Germany can only come into being from the Word of God in faith through the Holy Spirit. Only so does the Church become renewed."

In a not so subtle reference to the Nazification of the church, the declaration went on to acknowledge that the basic principles of the church were "systematically being thwarted and made ineffective by alien principles . . . when these principles are acknowledged . . . the church ceases to be the church."

The key paragraph that contradicted the popular teaching about the "two spheres" states: *"We reject the false doctrine that there are realms of our life in which we belong not to Jesus Christ, but to other masters, realms where we do not need to be justified and sanctified by*

Him"[12] (italics added). The role of the state, the leaders acknowledged, was to keep harmony and peace, but it was not to fulfill the church's vocation. No human sovereign should rule over the church; it must be under the Word of God to fulfill its role.

We must remember that this document did not criticize Nazism as a political movement; at this point, Germany had as yet not seen the worst of Hitler. Loyalty to the state was so deeply ingrained in the German soul that such a move would have been stoutly resisted by those who were present.

Though Niemöller and Bonhoeffer agreed that the church should be independent of the state, they disagreed about the nature of the Nazi regime. Early on, Bonhoeffer warned against Hitler's intentions and opposed his preparations for war. However, though Niemöller denounced Ludwig Müller from the chancel steps of his church, he did so with Nazi flags hanging on the walls and the Nazi salute being given by the congregation.

Loyalty to Hitler remained strong in the Confessing Church. The Barmen declaration said simply that the political sphere had no right to intrude in the spiritual sphere and that committed Christians were commanded to live out their faith in the whole of life. At this point the fervent hope was that both God and Caesar could be served without choosing between one or the other. Eventually that hope was shattered.

The church found it difficult (some would say impossible) to bring itself to resist political authority as long as it stayed in its "proper sphere." Only later would the church realize that blind obedience, even in the matters that belong to the state, might be a violation of the Christian mandate.

Many of our Christian heroes were lawbreakers. Whether it was John Bunyan, who sat in a Bedford jail for his preaching, or Richard Wurmbrand, who was beaten for teaching the Bible in Communist Romania, Christians have always insisted that there is a law that is higher than that of the state.

Conscientious objectors have for centuries disobeyed the state, believing that no Christian can participate in killing, even in a time of war. Every Christian must draw that line in accordance with his or her own convictions. But if we say that we will always obey the state, the state becomes our God. We can render unto Caesar that which is Caesar's only when we have rendered everything we have to God. These were the issues with which the German church wrestled.

If the Confessing Church had chosen to break away from the established Lutheran church and become a free church, it would have lost the financial support of the state. That was not a viable option since the Confessing Church declared that it was the true church whose spiritual heritage could be traced back to the Reformation. The "German Christians" insisted that *they* were the only legitimate church, believing that God was manifest in the course of German history and especially in the rise of Hitler. Thus the church was torn asunder from within.

Needless to say, the Barmen Confession caused a stir in Germany. Pastors who signed it, or were even found with a copy of it, were harassed by the Gestapo. Plans were made to terrorize the "dissenters."

When the "German Christians" held their own synod, Bonhoeffer did not attend. He simply could not bring himself to acknowledge them as a part of the true church. He wrote, "We have to fight for the true Church against the false Church of Antichrist . . . we are fighting for Christianity not only with regard to the Church in Germany but in the whole world. For everywhere on the earth are to be found those pagan and anti-Christian powers which appeared openly in our field."[13] If the truth is to be found in unity, he affirmed that unity can only be achieved through truth.

Thus the Protestants were divided into two groups, each claiming to constitute the church, each claiming to be the heirs of the Reformation. Many pastors were undecided; others hoped they could simply continue their ministries without choosing sides. Hitler, however, would not allow them the luxury of indecision. Eventually they would have to choose either Caesar or Christ. The swastika would not be content with dual allegiance.

The Confessing Church held a second synod that same year in Dahlem on October 20, 1934. Hitler's ruthlessness was no longer as skillfully hidden as it once was; so the convention declared, "The Reich church government has ruthlessly gone on destroying the church, invoking the authority of the Führer and drawing on the cooperation of political powers. . . . This means that a state of emergency exists and that the church has the right to act in order to remedy it."[14] Niemöller said clearly, "To obey these despots of the Church is to disobey God."

Declaring a "state of emergency" was a bold move indeed.

The Reich Church was condemned by the Synod, and the Synod pled for the church to wake up to the crisis of faith that was at hand. Unfortunately, however, little was done to follow up on this courageous affirmation. A request was made to the Reich bishop that he legitimize the right of the Confessing Church to exist, but it went unanswered. Persecution was stepped up with the charge that the Confessing Church was stirring up unrest among the people and inciting disloyalty to the state. Under such pressure, support for the Confessing Church began to erode.

DWINDLING SUPPORT

At its third synod held in Augsburg, the Confessing Church managed to skirt the major issues. No word was spoken about the need for the church to have the freedom to preach and teach the gospel. Hitler's "positive Christianity" and its implications were not addressed. Nor was a word spoken on behalf of the Jews.

EVEN WHEN THE CROSS WAS PREACHED, IT WAS AGAINST A BACKGROUND OF RESENTMENT TOWARD THE JEWS AND AN OVERWHELMING DESIRE TO BE GOOD GERMAN NATIONALISTS.

Bonhoeffer and Niemöller sent a letter to all the Confessing pastors calling upon them to stand firm. In part it read:

> It is our failure at this point which hangs like a curse over our Confessing Church. . . . This is a curse we have brought upon ourselves, for we have denied what God has entrusted to us. . . . Let us return and accept once more the binding character of these decisions [the two synods at Barmen and Dahlem]. Then we shall once more be clearly led. Let us not be oppressed by the fact that the Church's future appears to rest in what, to our eyes, seems to be impenetrable darkness; let it be enough for us to know what we are commanded to do.
>
> We are commanded to make a clear, uncompromising answer of No in the face of every temptation to solve the Church's problem in a way which contradicts the decisions of Barmen and Dahlem. May God

help us—if it come to the point—to be able to speak this *No,* gladly and in unity.[15]

The letter received little response. Many pastors still thought compromise was possible, hoping that Hitler would give the Confessing Church legitimacy in return for their quiet support of his military ventures and patriotism. Diplomacy, they hoped, would fare better than bold confrontation.

Bonhoeffer continued to stir up opposition to the National Church, which continued to seek the allegiance of the German people. He spoke openly about the anti-Semitism of the Reich and the dishonorable silence of the churches in the face of such injustice. "Where is Abel your brother?" he would ask.

Mounting unified opposition to the Nazis' treatment of Jews was impossible. The church was not merely neutral on the matter but quietly and often openly supported the ostracism of the Jews from the mainstream of German life. Here is a letter from a pastor to the editor of a German newspaper expressing gratitude for its stand on the Jewish question. In part it said:

> We stand enthusiastically behind your struggle against the Jewish death watch beetles which are undermining our Jewish nation. . . . So too against those friends of Jewry which are found even in the ranks of the Protestant pastorate. We will fight along side of you and we will not give up until the struggle against all Jewry and against the murderers of Our Savior has been brought to a victorious end, in the Spirit of Christ and of Martin Luther.
>
> In true fellowship, I greet you with Heil Hitler!
>
> Pastor Riechelmann[16]

Few pastors were willing to be brothers to the Jews. They were becoming weary of opposing the Nazi steamroller. Torn between God and Caesar, many pastors tried to serve both. They preached, taught, and sang hymns with swastikas still hanging in their churches. Even when the Cross was preached, it was against a background of resentment toward the Jews and an overwhelming desire to be good German nationalists.

Through crafty manipulation, the "German Christians" took the virtues of the church and turned them to their own use. By appealing to patriotism and pragmatic necessity, they rallied many undecided

Hitler Youth marching through the streets of Breslau during
the 1938 Sports Festival.

pastors to their banner. The Confessing Church began to lose its influence. Years later Bonhoeffer wrote in his *Ethics*, "If Evil appears in the form of light, benefit, loyalty and renewal, if it conforms with historical necessity and social justice, then this, if it is understood straightforwardly, is a clear proof of its abysmal wickedness."[17] The confession was still being made but not as loudly as it once was.

Hitler, of course, did not think Germany had room for two gods. Initially content with two crosses hung in the churches, in the end he insisted there be only one. Neither the cross of Christ nor the swastika could tolerate dual allegiance.

A choice would have to be made: Those who chose the Cross would have to walk a lonely road in one direction; those who chose the swastika would walk in step with the exuberant crowd. Those who chose the swastika participated in the fate of its leader; those who chose the cross of Christ discovered that "it is the power of God for salvation" (Romans 1:16).

Those choices still awaited the church that would yet have to be further refined.

CHAPTER SEVEN

THE CHURCH IS DISMEMBERED

E arly in 1934, Martin Niemöller mounted the pulpit of his church in the Berlin suburb of Dahlem and prophetically declared God's purpose in the trials that faced the German church:

> We have all of us—the whole Church and the whole community —we've been thrown into the Tempter's sieve, and he is shaking and the wind is blowing, and it must now become manifest whether we are wheat or chaff! Verily, a time of sifting has come upon us, and even the most indolent and peaceful person among us must see that the calm of a meditative Christianity is at an end. . . .
>
> It is now springtime for the hopeful and expectant Christian Church—it is testing time, and God is giving Satan a free hand, so he may shake us up and so that it may be seen what manner of men we are! . . .
>
> Satan swings his sieve and Christianity is thrown hither and thither; and he who is not ready to suffer, he who called himself a Christian only because he thereby hoped to gain something good for his race and his nation is blown away like chaff by the wind of this time.[1]

God let Satan loose to shake the whole German church to separate the wheat from the chaff. Christ did not abandon His people; if they would trust Him with their eternal souls He would walk with them through the fire of affliction. Christ had promised that He would build His church and "the gates of Hades would not prevail against it." The church, however small or humanly weak, would prevail.

We should not be surprised that God often judges the church severely. To the church at Ephesus that had lost its first love Christ sent a warning, "Repent and do the deeds you did at first; or else I am coming to you, and will remove your lampstand out of its place—unless you repent" (Revelation 2:5). The "lampstand" in the German church was, for the most part, wrested from its setting when the Cross before which all men should bow was exchanged for the cross by which proud men marched.

Near the end of this chapter we will be introduced to a German theologian who will tell us that the forces of wickedness were unleashed in Nazi Germany because the cross of Christ had been cast down. The church, he believed, was crushed on the rock called God, because "God is not mocked." And when the Cross was confused with the swastika, it no longer was "the power of God for salvation."

Even in judgment, there was mercy. Many true believers experienced the strength of Christ as He sustained them, comforting, empowering, and purifying. In some churches prayer meetings and evangelism continued. The church was not destroyed, though it was purged and its numbers were seen to be fewer than expected.

Bonhoeffer, for one, continued his courageous insistence that the church should return to Christ. In January 1936, he spoke to a meeting of the Confessing pastors for the last time. In the face of dwindling support, he pled with the leaders to return to their mission, regardless of the cost. Some of his students who were present at the meeting were later criticized for their outbursts during the discussion. That criticism was used by some to discredit everything Bonhoeffer said and stood for. He replied that these matters were trivial in comparison to the crisis the church faced: "Something very much more serious is at stake, namely the necessity that God's word alone shall have authority."[2]

Bonhoeffer could not bring himself to respect those pastors who continued to support the "German Christians." He understood the pressure to compromise but urged those charged with the responsibility of preaching the gospel to remain firm. He recounted that one of his own students had chosen to leave the Confessing Church and identify with the Reich Church. Bonhoeffer had spent hours in discussion with him, pointing out that to turn back was to turn his back on Christ. He was deeply hurt when the student chose to follow the path of compromise.

He was also disappointed that so few were willing to pay the price of fidelity to the gospel of God. Though he felt very much alone, he was unbowed, believing the Reich Church had become apostate. "I must say that, in my opinion, anyone who subjects himself to the Church Committees [of the Reich Church] in any way cannot remain a member of our Church."

THE FINAL STEPS OF DECLINE

After 1936 the church experienced dwindling hope and an avalanche of despair. Many wavered in their commitment to Christ as persecution increased. But some members of the Confessing Church continued to mount whatever protest they could.

A MEMO TO HITLER

In May 1936, the leadership of the Confessing Church sent a memo to Hitler, asking him to answer directly whether "the attempt to de-Christianize the German people is to become the official policy of the Government." It courageously stated, "Where Aryan man is glorified, God's Word witnesses to the fallenness of all men; where anti-semitism is forced on the Christian in the contest of the National Socialist weltanschauung [worldview], obligating him to hate the Jews, the Christian command to love one's neighbor points in the opposite direction." The memo listed instances of how the state had intruded into the life of the church, attempting to replace Christianity with the ideology of Nazism. It concluded with exhortations that Hitler could not misunderstand:

> Even an exalted cause must in the end lead the nation to ruin if it sets itself against the revealed will of God. God's church will endure, even if in the attempt to de-Christianize the German people millions of Evangelical Christians must forfeit their salvation. . . . Our people threaten to transgress the limits set it by God. [Nazism] seeks to make itself the measure of all things. That is human arrogance, setting itself up against God.[3]

Hitler ignored the memo, but when it was later "leaked" to the foreign press, he chose to respond. The Gestapo was sent on a rampage to round up the pastors of the Confessing Church. Eventually more than eight hundred pastors were arrested, and at least a few died in concentration camps. No one could seriously think that compromise was still possible.

Dr. Kerrl, a friend of Hitler who succeeded Ludwig Müller as Reich bishop, finally admitted that Hitler's "positive Christianity" was quite different from that of the historic faith. "No, Christianity is not dependent upon the Apostle's Creed. . . . True Christianity is represented by the party, and the German people are now called by the party and especially the Führer to real Christianity. . . . The Führer is the herald of a new revelation."[4]

This "new revelation" would attempt to destroy the old. Hitler would replace Christ. The new messiah would not tolerate any other gods before him.

THE IMPRISONMENT OF NIEMÖLLER

In June 1937, Dr. Niemöller preached his last sermon during the days of the Third Reich. He said in part, "We have no more thought of using our own powers to escape the arm of the authorities than had the Apostles of old. No more are we ready to keep silent at man's behest when God commands us to speak. For it is, and must remain, the case that we must obey God rather than man." Within a few days, he was arrested and imprisoned.

His congregation supported him by their care for his wife, Frau Niemöller, and their prayers. From the day of his arrest until the war ended, prayer services were held in his church daily. On one occasion when a large service was planned, the Gestapo locked the church doors. The crowd arranged themselves in front of the church, and finally after a long column was formed they sang Luther's ancient hymn *Ein feste Burg ist unser Gott* ("A Mighty Fortress Is Our God").

Niemöller's trial began on February 7, 1938. During the previous seven months he had been in solitary confinement. The indictments against him comprised fourteen typewritten pages. He was described as "one of the most extreme members of the Confessing Church." He was accused of speaking against the Reich with "malicious and provocative criticism . . . of a kind calculated to undermine the confidence of the People in their political leaders." He had violated the Law for the Prevention of Treacherous Attacks on State and Party. Thus he was charged with "Abuse of Pulpit." It was a simple case of "political" disloyalty.

In his biography *Pastor Niemöller,* Dietmar Schmidt tells the story of how a green-uniformed official escorted Niemöller from his prison cell to the courtroom. Alone with his escort he walked, filled with dread and loneliness. Niemöller knew that the outcome of the proceedings was a foregone conclusion. Where were his family and friends? Where were the members of the Confessing Church who had stood with him?

At that moment he experienced one of the most uplifting experiences of his life. His escort had so far not uttered a word but walked with regular footsteps, his face impassive. As they passed through the underground tunnel and were about to walk up the last flight of stairs, Niemöller heard a voice that seemed to be repeating a set of words, but it was so low it was difficult to know where it was coming from because of the echo. Then he realized it was his escort repeating, "The name of the Lord is a strong tower; the righteous runs into it and is safe" (Proverbs 18:10).

Niemöller was climbing the steps by then and gave no sign that he had heard the words. But his fear was gone and, says Schmidt, "in its place was the calm brilliance of an utter trust in God." The first thing Niemöller saw when he entered the courtroom was a picture of Adolf Hitler on the wall behind the judge's rostrum. Once or twice during the next few days, Niemöller caught a glimpse of the guard in the green uniform, but he never did see his face. The man would never know how much those words meant to his prisoner in the days ahead.[5]

TO THE END OF HIS LIFE HE FOUGHT, IN THE WORDS OF HIS FRIEND DIETRICH BONHOEFFER, "FOR THE CHURCH [TO] BE THE CHURCH."

Niemöller was sentenced to prison and then confined in concentration camps, ending up in Dachau where he remained until liberated by Allied troops. His commitment cost him seven years of suffering in a concentration camp. What is more surprising is that his suffering did not end when he was released after the war. There was still another chapter of his life to be written.

In a famous 1945 *Stuttgart Declaration of Guilt,* Niemöller led the Confessing Church to acknowledge the guilt it shared with the German people in the horrors of World War II. This provided an opportunity for the church worldwide to be reconciled with its German counterpart. For that action, however, Niemöller was denounced by his own countrymen as a traitor; many Germans, still believing Hitler's propaganda, blamed Britain, the United States, and particularly Russia for the fact that the flower of their youth had died in vain. Only later would they come to understand the magnitude of the Holocaust and their country's role in the war.

Meanwhile, Jewish leaders in the United States insisted that Niemöller never did condemn Nazism, but only its intrusion into the church. He was branded as one who was but "a little better than a Nazi." As the years went by, however, Niemöller's stature increased as a courageous Christian leader. To the end of his life he fought, in the words of his friend Dietrich Bonhoeffer, "for the church [to] be the church." Though he died in 1984, he still speaks to us today:

> First, they came for the socialists, and I did not speak out because I was not a socialist. Then they came for the trade unionists, and I did not speak out because I was not a trade unionist. Then they came for the Jews, and I did not speak out because I was not a Jew. Then they came for me, and there was no one left to speak out for me.[6]

Thankfully, Niemöller did speak out.

SWEARING ALLEGIANCE TO HITLER

The August 6, 1938, *Chicago Tribune* carried the headline "Bible Twisted to Nazi Creed." The article tells how the Sermon on the Mount and the gospel of John had been rewritten by former Reich Bishop Ludwig Müller. The words *sin* and *grace* were deleted from the texts, and the Golden Rule was rewritten to apply only to relationships between Nazi comrades. All references to Old Testament prophets, from Moses to Abraham, were also deleted. Everlasting life was defined as "true life."

A Nazified Christ approved German nationalism and the expansion of the German empire. This Christ was not concerned about eternal life, but about life today—the life of the average German citizen.This Christ had a different cross and a different future. He was Hitler, the one whom Dietrich Eckart had anointed as Antichrist.

A small group of Confessing Church leaders who foresaw the great danger of war circulated a statement that encouraged the churches to have services of intercession for their country and plead for the forgiveness of God. When a copy fell into Himmler's hands he published it, interpreting it as a "stab in the back" of Hitler's successes and branded the document "high treason." Fearing that they would be seen as unpatriotic, more pastors resigned from the Confessing Church.

Organized opposition to Hitler became all but impossible in the face of his foreign policy triumphs. In March of 1936, he reclaimed the Rhineland, which had been taken from Germany with the Treaty of Versailles. When he swiftly and successfully annexed Austria two years later in March of 1938, the Germans were ecstatic with the *Anschluss* (union with Austria). The Cardinal Archbishop of Vienna expressed support, urging that in upcoming church elections the people should vote for bishops who "confess themselves as Germans in the German Reich." The Protestants also expressed their loyalty. When German-speaking Czechoslovakia was seized, the church either supported the move or remained silent in the midst of the national euphoria.

Riding on the wave of enthusiasm generated by the annexation of Austria, Dr. Werner, Hitler's new deputy for church activities, sent a notice to all the pastors, stipulating that they must sign an oath of loyalty to Hitler as a personal birthday gift to him. The oath read in part, "I swear that I will be faithful and obedient to Adolf Hitler, the Führer of the German Reich and people, that I will conscientiously observe the laws and carry out the duties of my office so help me God." A further explanation said it was to be interpreted as meaning "the most intimate solidarity with the Third Reich . . . and with the man who created the community that embodies it . . . an oath of personal loyalty." To refuse the oath meant dismissal, or worse.

During Holy Week, the cross on the Wartburg Castle where Luther had hidden to evade his enemies was replaced by an immense, floodlit swastika. The bishop of the area sent a telegram to Hitler reporting that a great historic hour had arrived. All the pastors in his district had obeyed an inward command and "have with joyful hearts taken an oath of loyalty to Führer and Reich . . . One God, One obedience to the faith. Hail my Führer!"[7] Other districts followed the same "inward command."

At first the pastors of the Confessing Church refused to comply. On the one hand they did not want to violate their consciences; yet they also wanted to be patriotic to the German state. When the Confessing Church met in June of 1938 to respond to the latest crisis, many of the pastors had already taken the oath, attempting to interpret it as simply an extension of their ordination vows.

Those pastors who had not signed the oath—bless them!—came seeking guidance on how they could continue to stand together against the Nazi threat. However, the synod, demoralized by fear, refused to fight against the political firestorm that now engulfed them. The majority overruled the minority and did that which could only gladden the heart of Hitler himself: They decided that individual pastors and church leaders should make up their own minds about taking the oath of loyalty. That decision had disastrous consequences. It made it easy for the Gestapo to identify any pastor who didn't comply, arrest him, and sentence him to whatever the People's Court would decide.

Thus many of the remaining pastors of the Confessing Church joined with those who had capitulated and took the oath of loyalty. Bonhoeffer was crushed. It was a "gash in his own flesh" that was inflicted by his own people. He felt the shame one would have for his own family. "Will the Confessing Church be willing to confess publicly its guilt and disunion?" he asked. At last the choice was unmistakably clear: *In bowing to the swastika, the pastors turned their backs on the Cross.*

The few who didn't sign the oath joined the eight hundred who had previously been rounded up in accordance with Hitler's wishes. Perhaps a few were still able to evade Hitler's edict, but not many. It was a time, says one, "when the power of darkness was greater than the power of light."

J. S. Conway wrote, "Under a barrage of accusations and vilification, the Confessing Church members grew more and more confused between their political and their theological loyalties. Their resolution weakened and their morale sank to its lowest ebb."[8] Poised between two crosses, divided by compromise, and weakened through internal theological differences, the Confessing Church lost its collective influence.

In the summer of 1938, the head of the Gestapo could say in his annual report, "The situation in the Churches is characterized by weariness with the struggle, by uncertainty of purpose and by lack of courage."[9] Hitler had managed to marginalize the church, to reduce its flame to a flicker. The Protestant "dogs," as he called them, were for the most part submissive.

Those pastors who took the oath were allowed to continue their ministries, but they had to be loyal to the Nazi ideology. A few months later in November 1938 when, under the leadership of Goebbels, the notorious "Crystal Night" attack was launched against the Jews, the church was largely silent. Despite the burning of 177 synagogues and the arrest of twenty thousand Jews in a land where 95 percent of the people belonged either to the Catholic or Protestant church, the leaders chose to look the other way. "They fell silent" says Conway, "even in the face of such monstrous outrages." A Catholic bishop in Berlin who led his people in prayer for the Jews was imprisoned and later died in a concentration camp.

IF ONLY THE CHURCH HAD SEEN THAT WHEN THE JEWS WERE PERSECUTED IT WAS THE LORD JESUS WHO WAS SUFFERING!

Let us not overlook the hundreds of pastors who did not take the oath of loyalty to Hitler. They became witnesses for Christ in the prisons and concentration camps. When the war was over survivors told of being upheld by those whose faith in God was tested and found to withstand the onslaught. Only God knows how many Jews and Gentiles were converted because of their testimony. Though we can often see the judgment that God inflicts upon His church, the purification is hidden from us. The chaff is more easily seen than the wheat, which is most precious to Him.

We salute those who accepted imprisonment and even death rather than the suppression of their freedoms. We honor those faithful families who continued to instruct their children in the face of bitter opposition. We honor all who did not bow their knees to a lesser god. The price they paid makes their courage and love all the greater. God shall reward them.

THE RESPONSE OF THE PEOPLE

What did the rest of Germany think of the news that eight hundred pastors were arrested and imprisoned for not accepting the Nazification of their churches? What was the response to the fact that thousands of pastors had sworn personal allegiance to Hitler? The people were apathetic.

William Shirer, in his monumental *The Rise and Fall of the Third Reich,* gives one of the most chilling assessments of the values Germans held dear. Though this paragraph is long, I encourage you to read every word. Shirer writes:

> It would be misleading to give the impression that the persecution of Protestants and Catholics by the Nazi State tore the German people asunder or even greatly aroused the vast majority of them. It did not. A people who had so lightly given up their political and cultural and economic freedoms were not, except for a relatively few, going to die or even risk imprisonment to preserve freedom of worship. What really aroused the Germans in the Thirties were the glittering successes of Hitler in providing jobs, creating prosperity, restoring Germany's military might, and moving from one triumph to another in his foreign policy. Not many Germans lost much sleep over the arrests of a few thousand pastors and priests or over the quarreling of the various Protestant sects. And even fewer paused to reflect that under the leadership of Rosenberg, Bormann, and Himmler, who were backed by Hitler, the Nazi regime intended eventually to destroy Christianity in Germany, if it could, and substitute the old paganism of the early tribal Germanic gods and the new paganism of the Nazi extremists. As Bormann, one of the men closest to Hitler, said publicly in 1941, "National socialism and Christianity are irreconcilable."[10]

So there you have it. The majority of the people, including the professing Christians, no longer believed that Christianity was worth suffering for, much less dying for. They were willing to substitute *Mein Kampf* for the Bible in exchange for jobs and the greater glory of Germany. Yet those who saved their lives lost them, and those who lost their lives saved them.

What might have happened if the church had condemned Nazism with one unified voice? In a sermon in 1945, Niemöller gave what could be a kind of epilogue on the German church struggle. He said,

There were in 1933 and in the following years here in Germany 14,000 Evangelical pastors and nearly as many parishes. . . . If at the beginning of the Jewish persecutions we had seen that it was the Lord Jesus Christ who was being persecuted, struck down and slain in "the least of these our brethren," if we had been loyal to Him and confessed Him, for all I know God would have stood by us, and then the whole sequence of events would have taken a different course. And if we had been ready to go with Him to death, the number of victims might well have been only some ten thousand.[11]

Yes, if only the church had seen that when the Jews were persecuted it was the Lord Jesus who was suffering! Jesus, when referring to the Tribulation period, said that the King will say to those who inherit the kingdom, "For I was hungry, and you gave Me something to eat; I was thirsty, and you gave Me drink; I was a stranger, and you invited Me in; naked, and you clothed Me; I was sick, and you visited Me; I was in prison, and you came to Me" (Matthew 25:35–36).

And when the righteous cannot recall having done those things for Christ, they will hear from His own lips, "Truly I say to you, to the extent that you did it to one of these brothers of Mine, even the least of them, you did it to Me" (v. 40). Yes, the Jews were Christ to the Christians in Germany; so were the pastors who went into prison; so were the children who were drafted to fight a cruel war.

When the war began in 1939, persecution of the churches abated. Hitler knew that he needed the sons of the church to fight under the Nazi banner. Thus many of the churches and their congregations continued to hold services and prayer meetings at the same time that they sent their sons to battle in "Hitler's War." Caesar was calling, and the Germans responded.

After years of studying Hitler's persecution of the church, J. S. Conway wrote, "The illusion that Hitler could do no wrong, even if his subordinates openly persecuted the Church and clergy, faded only when events in the last years of the war forced all Germans to see that their idol had feet of clay."[12]

WHAT WENT WRONG?

In April 1945, amid the ruins of a defeated Germany, Helmut Thielicke, a German theologian and pastor, spoke movingly to his congregation in Stuttgart about the meaning of all that had happened. In a message that surely must have left his congregation spellbound, he in effect said that the nation got what it deserved because it had "repudiated forgiveness and kicked down the cross of the Lord."[13]

In his powerful critique of what had gone wrong in a nation that was "Christian," Thielicke said that the cross of Christ had been neglected and thus the church was blinded to Germany's militarism. The church had overlooked its greatest danger, namely, that in gaining the whole world it might "lose its own soul." Wherein was the failure? Thielicke lists the mistakes:

- That this people would think they themselves are making history, . . . whereas they are only blind horses led of God.

- That this people should consider itself a chosen people, whereas the fist of God has already raised to dash it to the ground.

- That in its temporal tasks the church should disregard the Eternal and in its faith in itself fail to see its guilt and need for forgiveness.

- That this people should imagine that it believes in God, whereas they are the victim of the devil and his shimmering soap bubbles.

- That this people should proceed with fanatical energy to solve economic, social, and political problems and in solving these problems overlook or simply ignore the fact that first and foremost we need a Redeemer, who would set straight the deepest basis of our personal lives.

- That we were unaware of the dangers on which we have been shipwrecked—shipwrecked by being blind to the most terrible danger: namely, there is a devil who can lead a man about by the nose in the midst of all his idealism, and there is a God upon whom we can wreck ourselves because "He is not mocked."

- That we did not calculate the factor that is called "God" in our plans and therefore fell victims to megalomania.

- That we violated God's commandments and got tangled in our own unpredictable and brutal instincts.

- That we ignored that monumental call "I am the Lord your God, you shall have no other gods before me" and hence landed in a giddy ecstasy of power worship that brought the whole world against us.

- That we ceased to trust ourselves to the miracle of God's guidance and therefore we put our faith instead in miracle weapons that never came.

• That we no longer knew that God is in heaven and man is on earth, and thus we lost all sense of the proportions of life and consequently were stricken with blindness in purely external political and military relationships.

Thielicke then came to the heart of the matter: "Denying God and casting down the cross is never a merely private decision that concerns only my own inner life and my personal salvation, but this denial immediately brings the most brutal consequences for the whole of historical life and especially for our own people. 'God is not mocked.' The history of the world can tell us terrible tales based on that text."

In history, he says, the invisible is mightier and more creative and destructive than the visible. Anybody who still had not grasped that Germany with its program "was wrecked precisely on this dangerous rock called 'God' and nothing else has no eyes to see. Because he sees only individual catastrophes he no longer sees the basic, cardinal catastrophe behind them all."

Finally, he reminded his listeners that "the worship of success is generally the form of idol worship the devil cultivates most assiduously. . . . We could observe in the first years after 1933 the almost suggestive compulsion that emanates from great successes and how under the influence of these successes even Christians stopped asking in whose name and at what price they were achieved. . . . Success is the greatest narcotic of all."

Casting down the cross of Christ! Intoxicated with success! Substituting the temporary for the permanent! Thus was the church and the entire country crushed, crushed on the rock called God "who is not mocked." Destroyed for being blinded by the pride of nationalism instead of being humbled by its great need for repentance. The church stood with pride, but it would not bow in humility.

DID THE GATES OF HADES PREVAIL?

What do we make of Hitler's apparent victory in crushing the church? Did the "gates of Hades" prevail? To put the question differently, Did God win, even in Nazi Germany? Yes, God always wins, even when He appears to lose. *He does not have to win numerically to win spiritually.*

The question is not how many souls are saved; nor is it the number who were willing to suffer for their faith. Jesus was under no illusion about the percentage of those who would turn out to be His true followers. "Do not be afraid, little flock, for your Father has chosen gladly to give you the kingdom" (Luke 12:32). The great kingdom goes to the "little flock."

There have been times in world history, particularly in medieval times, when the light of the gospel was practically extinguished. Apart from several small persecuted groups and those relatively few individuals who experienced the personal saving grace of Christ, the gospel was hidden under centuries of tradition. Even then, God always had His people, for "the Lord knoweth them that are His."

Christ's mission could not possibly fail. He taught that there were certain people whom the Father had given to Him as a gift. The salvation of these would be absolutely certain, for the Father would draw them and Christ would receive them. "All that the Father gives Me shall come to Me, and the one who comes to Me I will certainly not cast out" (John 6:37).

IF EVERY PASTOR HAD BEEN A BONHOEFFER OR A NIEMÖLLER, TEXTBOOKS ON GERMAN HISTORY MIGHT READ DIFFERENTLY TODAY.

When Paul the apostle explained to the church at Rome that Christ was the Messiah, many people asked, Has God not failed? After all, He promised blessing to the Jews, and since they rejected His Son, it appears as if God's power and integrity are tarnished.

To those who thought that the plan of God had fizzled, Paul wrote, "But it is not as though the word of God has failed" (Romans 9:6). Literally, the Greek phrase could be translated, "It is not as though the word of God is off course." The lostness of Israel does not mean that God's plans have been frustrated. In the rest of chapter 9 Paul argues that God is saving those whom He planned to save; hence His plan is perfectly successful. God wins because everything is orchestrated according to His own purpose.

People were being converted even during the dark days of Nazi Germany. God was drawing His people to Himself and purifying His church. Some genuine believers buckled under the pressure of the Nazi threats, but we read in Scripture, "If we are faithless, He remains faithful; for He cannot deny Himself" (2 Timothy 2:13). God was walking through the fire with His people. God was willing to have the clouds of chaff blown away for the kernels of wheat, however many or few, that remained.

Let us remember that *God does not have to win in time in order to win in eternity.* Many battles on earth appear to be won by Satan; but the more he wins now, the greater his defeat later on. God has all of eternity to prove who is greater. In fact, if Satan were wise, he would cease all rebellion against God immediately since he will be judged for his anarchy. The more battles he wins here, the greater his judgment in the future. In the end he is thrown into the lake of fire. The fight isn't over until the bell rings.

In addition, *God needs only acknowledgment, not allegiance.* Every created being will acknowledge that Jesus Christ is Lord. "That at the name of Jesus every knee should bow, of those who are in heaven, and on earth, and under the earth, and that every tongue should confess that Jesus Christ is Lord, to the glory of God the Father" (Philippians 2:10–11). This admission of truth, even on the part of proud men and the satanic hosts, will bring glory to God.

Obviously those who are in eternal torment, whether a sinful human or a fallen angel, will never come to love God and enjoy His fellowship. But the truth will triumph; every lie will be exposed. Justice shall reign, and God shall be glorified.

Many believers in Germany lost a remarkable opportunity to display the power of God, while others were given a remarkable opportunity to display a faith that was most precious to God. If every pastor had been a Bonhoeffer or a Niemöller, textbooks on German history might read differently today. Perhaps Niemöller was right: God might have prevented Hitler from carrying out the Holocaust. Nevertheless, God wins even when the church appears to lose. When Satan casts down the cross of Christ, it is only for a time. In the end all rival crosses will prove to be broken indeed.

Peter Marshall said, "It is better to fail in a cause that will ultimately succeed, than to succeed in a cause that will ultimately fail."

Better to fail within the church than to be successful outside of it. Better to be a part of a small crowd that appears to lose now but wins later than to belong to a large crowd whose victories are temporary and illusionary.

Niemöller and Bonhoeffer were not the only heroes in the Third Reich. In fact, there were thousands of heroes, more than we will ever know. These were the courageous ones who helped the Jews, took risks in standing for the gospel, and were even willing to try to overthrow Hitler.

The question we will try to answer in the next chapter is, What is the profile of a hero? Would we have been heroes if we had lived in Germany then?

CHAPTER EIGHT

HEROISM IN THE THIRD REICH

W e have often been critical of the church in Nazi Germany, but the famous physicist Albert Einstein was impressed with its struggle against Hitler. Though the failings of the church have been well documented, Einstein paid tribute to it as the only institution that provided sustained opposition to the Nazi regime. As Hitler's darker side was revealed, a large section of the population began to resist his policies. Thousands of ordinary Christians (along with those who would not want to classify themselves as such) helped rescue the Jews from their fate.

Einstein, exiled from Germany because he was a Jew, wrote:

> Being a lover of freedom, when the [Nazi] revolution came I looked to the universities to defend it, knowing that they had always boasted of their devotion to the cause of truth; but no, the universities were immediately silenced. Then I looked to the great editors of the newspapers, whose flaming editorials in days gone by had proclaimed their love of freedom; but they, like the universities, were silenced in a few short weeks.
>
> Only the Church stood squarely across the path of Hitler's campaign for suppressing the truth. I never had any special interest in the Church before, but now I feel a great affection and admiration for it

because the Church alone has had the courage and persistence to stand for intellectual and moral freedom. I am forced to confess that what I once despised I now praise unreservedly.[1]

Swiss theologian Karl Barth gave a balanced assessment of the role of the church: "In proportion to its task, the Church has sufficient reason to be ashamed that it did not do more; yet in comparison with those of other groups and institutions it has no reason to be ashamed; it accomplished more than all the rest."[2] The church might not have done all it *should* have done or *could* have done, but it did something! In the final analysis, there were heroes in Germany; there were many who took the risk to withstand the moral bankruptcy of a Nazi regime.

Suffering purifies the church; it makes important distinctions among men. When I was in China in 1984, Bishop Ding of the Three Self Movement told some of us candidly, "Persecution wiped out theological liberalism in China. . . . The church in China today is largely evangelical." In our day, as in every era, the church that preaches a Christ who is worth dying for has the best chance of experiencing persecution but also the best chance of survival. False Christs are unworthy of the ultimate sacrifice; only the Christ of the New Testament can ask for our highest loyalty.

Of course, the apostate church and true believers suffered together in Germany. But the latter had the promises of Christ to sustain them during the sifting process. The church had to learn the same lessons that the church has had to learn throughout the two thousand years of its turbulent history. "Beloved, do not be surprised at the fiery ordeal among you, which comes upon you for your testing, as though some strange thing were happening to you; but to the degree that you share the sufferings of Christ, keep on rejoicing; so that . . . you may rejoice with exultation" (1 Peter 4:12–13).

Jerome, a fourth-century scholar, wrote, "The church of Christ has been founded by shedding its own blood, not that of others; by enduring outrage, not by inflicting it. Persecutions have made it grow; martyrdoms have crowned it." Suffering gives the church its credibility.

Sometimes the gospel has to be communicated with more than words. Michael Baumgarten, a nineteenth-century Lutheran pastor who was excommunicated from his church, wrote, "There are times in which lectures and publications no longer suffice to communicate the necessary truth. At such times the deeds and sufferings of the saints must create a new alphabet in order to reveal again the secret of truth."[3]

Suffering communicates the gospel in a new language; it authenticates the syllables that flow so easily from our lips. Bonhoeffer warned the church that it had to be ready to suffer, even to the point of death. In a sermon in the Kaiser-Wilhelm Memorial Church in Berlin he said, "We must not be surprised if once again times return for our church when the blood of the martyrs will be required." In somber reflection he continued, "But even if we have the courage and faith to spill it, this blood will not be as innocent or as clear as that of the first martyrs. Much of our own guilt will lie in our blood. The guilt of the useless servant who is thrown into the darkness."[4]

Yes, the blood that was shed by believers in Nazi Germany was not as innocent and clear as that of the first martyrs. The church in Germany, Bonhoeffer believed, was persecuted as judgment for its own sins. The foreign cross that adorned its cathedrals was proof that the message of spiritual redemption had been replaced by a message of political expansion.

A few years ago I was in a Muslim country where there are about two hundred genuine converts to Christianity in total. An American Christian observed, and I believe that the Muslim converts would agree, that the church will not grow in such countries until the believers are willing to be publicly identified and suffer. Suffering gives the Cross its most enduring witness. *When the chaff is separated from the wheat, the wheat germinates and begins to grow.*

Those of us who live in America think that suffering for Christ is somehow fundamentally inadmissible; it is un-American and contradicts the notion that I should do "what is best for me." As a result of our aversion to this badge of honor, Christian students in our universities, fearing the consequences of disagreeing with "politically correct" agendas, often fall silent about their faith in Christ to avoid stirring the academic waters so that they will be permitted to graduate.

An InterVarsity campus minister told a reporter for *Christianity Today* that "Christians are not singled out unless they believe there is a hell or talk about abortion." The reason, he says, that attacks against Christians at the university seldom get personal is that very few students are willing to jeopardize their status by defending their views. Nathan Chan, a Christian enrolled at Stanford Graduate School, said, "If you take [multiculturalism] to an extreme it is very individualistic, you have your own bias, and you can think what you want in that box, so long as you don't affect others' boxes. When you say that Christianity is the only truth, you are imposing on someone's box."5

But if Christians are silent at our universities for fear of being disgraced; if believers are intimidated at work because of new laws that might keep religion out of the workplace; if a Christian nurse is silent about abortion because to speak out would put her job in jeopardy; in short, *if we keep Christ to ourselves out of fear of reprisals, are we not taking our stand with those pastors in Germany who chose to close ranks with Hitler?* Is not our sin even greater since the consequences of our obedience to Christ are so minimal in comparison with what they faced? Are we qualified to sit in judgment of the church in Germany if we ourselves have never lost a job or failed a course because we are Christians?

LET'S SEE HOW GOD KEPT HIS PROMISES AND THEN ASK: WHAT IS THE PROFILE OF A HERO? WOULD WE QUALIFY?

The prophet Jeremiah wrote, "If you have run with footmen and they have tired you out, then how can you compete with horses? If you fall down in a land of peace, how will you do in the thicket of the Jordan?" (Jeremiah 12:5). If we can't be loyal to Christ in the small decisions, how can we expect to be loyal when our faith might cost us something very precious?

Only when we see value in the lesser sacrifice will we be willing to be faithful in the greater one. Only when we see why the pastors in Germany should have chosen prison will we be willing to be faithful to Christ even if a lawsuit is filed against us. Let us pass these tests so that we will be prepared for the tougher ones if they come.

HOW GOD KEPT HIS PROMISES
Here is the story of two men who found unexpected peace while awaiting death. I've adapted these stories from the helpful book *The Men Who Tried to Kill Hitler,* by Roger Manvell and Heinrich Fraenkel.

Dietrich Bonhoeffer.

Count Helmut James Moltke formed a resistance group, not so much to overthrow Hitler as to form a strategy of how to pick up the pieces when the war ended. Moltke was captured and faced his Nazi interrogator who told him, "Only in one respect does National Socialism resemble Christianity: we demand the whole man." To this, I believe, all of us would say, "*Ja wohl!*"

Many of Moltke's farewell letters have survived; they were written to his wife and smuggled out of the Tegel prison. He wrote in hourly expectation of death, explaining repeatedly to his wife that he was never in better spirits nor felt so close to God. He said he expected that in the closing hours of a man's life he would be thinking, *This is the last time you will see the sun go down; or the last time you will go to bed,* but he was in an exalted state and felt in the best of spirits. He continues:

> I can only pray to our Heavenly Father that he will keep me in this state, since to die thus is obviously easier for the flesh. How good God has been to me! I must risk sounding hysterical, but I am so filled with

gratitude that there's really room for nothing else. His guidance of men was so sure and clear during these two days. Had the whole court been in an uproar, had Herr Freisler and the surrounding walls tottered before my eyes, it would have made no difference to me.[6]

Moltke wrote that when he and his wife shared Communion together in his cell, he wept out of gratitude because he was overwhelmed by the presence of God. Though he could not yet see God face-to-face he said, "He has gone before us as a cloud by day and as a fire by night. . . . Now nothing further can happen." He was hanged days later, and it was reported that he "went on his way steadfast and calm."

Fabian von Schlabrendorf was a young lawyer who opposed Hitler from the beginning. He was not particularly religious, at least not until he was tortured. The torture to which he was subjected that information might be extracted from him is chilling indeed. His hands were locked finger by finger behind his back and spikes were injected into his fingertips. The second stage was the confinement of his thighs and legs in a special apparatus so that he was strapped down on a bedlike frame; then by means of screws, sharp points were driven into his limbs. The third stage was the medieval stretching on a frame that expanded the strapped body either gradually or in agonizing jerks. The fourth stage was to beat the victim with heavy clubs so that his body, trussed up in a bent position, constantly fell forward with the full weight on the face and head.

The commissioner himself administered the tortures, laughing and sneering as he did so. Only when Schlabrendorf lost consciousness did the torturing stop. When he recovered, he was tortured again. He knew that other prisoners were being treated in the same way and afterward wrote:

> We all made the discovery that a man can endure far more pain than he would have deemed possible. Those of us who never learned to pray did so now, and found that prayer and only prayer can bring comfort in such terrible straits, and it gives more than human endurance. We learned also that the prayers of our friends and relatives could transmit currents of strength to us.[7]

Prayer transmitted currents of strength! Both of those men had taken the risk of opposing Hitler and faced the consequences. Though they were ordinary men they found extraordinary grace at the time of need.

One father wrote a note to his family, giving a final farewell to his wife and children individually. He concludes "Dearest ones! Don't cry for me—I am happy and protected. The alpine roses, your last sweet greeting from our beloved mountains stand withered before me. In two hours I shall enter into the true freedom of the heights, for which I have been struggling for a life time."[8] He ends with a prayer, then signs simply, "Your loving Father."

In his book *Bonhoeffer: Exile and Martyr,* Eberhard Bethge points out that martyrs stand apart from those who die as victims of the wrath of others. Martyrdom has distinctive characteristics.[9]

First, the risk of martyrdom is freely chosen. The Jews who died in concentration camps were not martyrs in the classical sense of the word. They were victims by virtue of their name and birth; it did not matter what they did or didn't do. Their enemies chose suffering for them.

In contrast, martyrs choose the path of suffering in the face of other options. They could have denied their convictions or remained silent. But they spoke out or acted, choosing to obey God rather than man. They understood the risks, but did it anyway.

We have already met two such heroes, but there were thousands of others in Germany and other countries. In *The Holocaust: A History of Courage and Resistance,* the author tells how a young beautiful French woman, Lisa, carried funds, documents, or weapons on her bicycle to those who were in hiding.[10] Another girl journeyed into the woods to find Jews who might be hiding so that they could be fed. Isaac was a young man who stayed up all night printing leaflets with important information for those who suffered.

One brave woman secretly wrote the outline of the Jewish seder that it might be unobtrusively observed in a concentration camp. In Paris some Frenchmen carried yellow handkerchiefs in their pockets and held the Star of David in their hands. For that they were sent to concentration camps and each forced to wear a white armband that read, "Jew Friend."

In Denmark almost all the Jews were hidden and their lives spared. Doctor Gersfelt gave children sleeping pills to keep them quiet while they were being transported to safety on fishing boats across a one-half mile waterway. Erin Kiaer, a bookbinder, took so many Jews to safety on fishing boats that he was hunted by the Nazis. Eventually, he was captured and tortured, but he never revealed any information. An ambulance driver, warned that a special roundup of Jews was about to begin, took Jews to a hospital where he knew they could be safely hidden.

In each of these cases and thousands more, individuals thought of creative ways to identify with the plight of the Jewish people. They risked their careers and even their lives to help those who were in need. When one couple was asked why they hid so many Jews, the wife replied, "It was like seeing a neighbor's house on fire. Naturally you want to help them." As one pastor put it, "I would rather die with the Jews than live with the Nazis."

The second characteristic of a true martyr is that he does not seek to die but is willing to accept death should it come. He might even greatly fear death, but he fears compromise much more. These people were not looking for death, hoping to be martyred for some noble deed. Most martyrs have a strong desire to live, and forfeit life only reluctantly.

Third, martyrs have a fanatical commitment to a cause that they regard to be more important than life itself. Some have been martyred for their religious commitment; others for seeking to overthrow a political regime. The students standing in front of the tanks in Tienanmen Square in China were martyred for the cause of freedom. Millions throughout the centuries have been martyred for Christ.

Finally, most martyrs believe that to remain silent is to comply with the enemy. They would agree with Abraham Lincoln that "silence makes cowards out of the best of men." This cowardice, martyrs affirm, is exactly what they labored to overcome. Even when given the option of silence, they are so overwhelmed by the greatness of the cause that they speak out or act as emissaries of justice.

Most discussions of the Holocaust speak of two groups of people—the Nazi perpetrators and the Jewish victims. There were also many bystanders who numbered in the millions, most of whom would have described themselves as Christians. The majority "sought refuge in neutrality." Yet whether we like to admit it or not, this neutrality was, in effect, complicity.

Bonhoeffer wrote in 1940 that the church had "become guilty of the deaths of the weakest and most defenseless brothers of Jesus Christ." He believed that the church must stand against injustice even if that injustice was directed to those outside the church. For him it was not enough to refuse to participate in a boycott against the Jews; it was necessary to actively take up their cause, to fight in their behalf and be identified with their concerns. The fact that the Jews were defenseless was even greater reason that the Christians should have stood at their side.

The non-Jews who risked their lives and the lives of their families to help Jews survive are called "the righteous Gentiles of the Holocaust." They hid the Jews, defended them, and stood with them in their trials. As Bonhoeffer taught, the suffering Jew was Christ suffering; the rejected child was Christ rejected.

These righteous Gentiles are honored as heroes in Israel and wherever the Holocaust is remembered. At the Holocaust Memorial and Museum in Jerusalem, thousands of evergreen trees have been planted in what is called "The Garden of the Righteous." Each tree represents a Gentile rescuer. More than eleven thousand Gentiles have been officially recognized. The total, however, might be as many as 100,000 Gentiles in Europe who acted to help Jews survive.

It is estimated that, on average, each rescuer helped one Jew escape death, so it might well be that 100,000 lives were spared because of these rescuers. Most of these rescuers were self-identified Christians. Even many Jews have wondered why Christians have not always honored those of our number who risked their lives for those who were despised.

Studies have been done to help us profile the rescuers, those who risked their lives to help others. These are the people you would have wanted as next-door neighbors if you were a Jew living in Nazi Germany. They are the people who believe that some things are more important than living comfortably when surrounded by injustice.

OF WHAT STUFF ARE HEROES MADE?

Obviously the heroes during the Nazi era were not all Christians. Many were nominally "Christian" while others perhaps had no faith at all. Certainly the Christians should have led the way; often they did, but sometimes they didn't.

What are the characteristics of those who refused to retreat into dishonorable silence? In *Christianity Today,* David P. Gushee revealed the results of his investigation into the kind of people who helped rescue the Jews.[11] First, they were diverse in their backgrounds: rich, poor, young, and old; an incongruity of social classes and education. They represented such a cross-section of Europe that those who would become rescuers "could not be predicted by any measure that sociologists use."

Second, there is some evidence to suggest that rescuers had a more stable home life than the bystanders. Many had parents who modeled the universal values of love and justice. They had a strong sense of social responsibility and capacity to empathize with suffering people. They show a consistent pattern of helping people before and after the Holocaust as well as during it.

A well-nigh universal trait of a rescuer was an unwillingness to accept praise for his or her deeds. "It is what anyone would have done," they said of behavior that not many did.

Third, they were motivated for a variety of reasons. A significant number had personal ties with the Jews they rescued. One woman said that she didn't get involved until her Jewish family doctor was targeted by the Gestapo. These friendships, for the most part formed before the Holocaust, bore fruit later on. As Christ said, "Greater love has no one than this, that one lay down his life for his friends" (John 15:13).

Others were motivated by group influence. Some saved Jews because of the moral example or exhortations of others. These groups might have been family, friends, or church. That is a reminder, says Gushee, that we are profoundly influenced by those whose opinions matter to us. We must "ask whether the church can recover its appropriate role as such a community of moral action and accountability."

"CAN THERE BE ANY DOUBT WHAT JESUS WOULD HAVE DONE IF A JEWISH FAMILY CAME TO HIS DOOR AND ASKED FOR HELP IN SURVIVING THE HOLOCAUST?"

Sometimes heroism was born as an immediate response to justice and compassion. Those who had a principled commitment to human rights and decency would be overcome by outrage in witnessing moral injustice. Their anger, mixed with sympathy, would motivate them to action.

Those who were specifically Christian said that they were sustained by the conviction that rescuing Jews was God's will. They were strengthened by prayer, Bible study, and the support of other Christians. They gained courage knowing that, if they were killed, they would stand before God with a clear conscience.

Gushee ends his study by asking, "Can there be any doubt what Jesus would have done if a Jewish family came to his door and asked for help in surviving the holocaust? We think we know the answer."

That leads me to ask, What would you or I have done if the Jews could have come to our door? I think that can be partly answered by asking another question: What are we doing now for those who come to our door—the poor, the person who has experienced discrimination, or the unwanted children (both born and unborn) in our land?

What would Christ do?

CHRIST'S ENCOURAGEMENT
TO THE PERSECUTED

Christ pronounced a blessing on those who would suffer for His name. "Blessed are you when men cast insults at you, and persecute you, and say all kinds of evil against you falsely, on account of Me. Rejoice, and be glad, for your reward in heaven is great, for so they persecuted the prophets who were before you" (Matthew 5:11–12). *Christians have every reason to be the first to volunteer when suffering is called for.*

First-century Smyrna, like the cities in twentieth-century Germany, was a town with a suffering church. It was not the place to be a Christian unless, of course, you were prepared to suffer. In fact, Christ predicted that some would pay for their faith with their lives. Though nineteen centuries separated those believers from the pastors in Germany, their choice was essentially the same.

To these frightened believers, Christ wrote a personal letter of encouragement:

And to the angel of the church in Smyrna write: The first and the last, who was dead, and has come to life, says this: "I know your tribulation and your poverty (but you are rich), and the blasphemy by those who say they are Jews and are not, but are a synagogue of Satan. Do not fear what you are about to suffer. Behold, the devil is about to cast some of you into prison, that you may be tested, and you will have tribulation ten days. Be faithful until death, and I will give you the crown of life. He who has an ear, let him hear what the Spirit says to the churches. He who overcomes shall not be hurt by the second death." (Revelation 2:8–11)

The source of the persecution, evidently, was the temple erected to Emperor Tiberius. The city had competed for the honor of building it and took pride in its construction. But the Christians would not sprinkle incense before it or declare "Caesar is Lord." Their refusal was viewed as disgraceful and unpatriotic. They knew that no church has room for two flags or two crosses.

Whereas Germany persecuted the Jews, in the Revelation account the Jews persecuted the Christians. The Jews were exempt from having to call Caesar Lord, so they were free to vilify the Christians who would not perform the sacred rituals. Christ said that those Jews were not really Jews but were from "the synagogue of Satan." That is, though they might have been Jews by blood, they were perverse in their dealings with others.

What was the result? First, the Christians faced poverty, probably because they were relegated to the lower rungs of society. No doubt they were too honest to get the easy profits that other merchants received through dishonest weights and measures. Others would not trade with them because they were Christians. Possibly some had their homes pillaged. Poverty was part of the burden they carried for their love for Christ.

Second, they experienced slander. "I know . . . the blasphemy by those who say they are Jews and are not" (v. 9). The Jews had circulated rumors; and their false accusations were akin to the attacks from the devil, whose name means "accuser." The Christians were hurt by the abuse.

Third, some were thrown into prison. "Behold, the devil is about to cast some of you into prison" (v. 10a). To quote John Stott, "The cells of Jerusalem and Caesarea, of Philippi and Rome, had been sanctified by the prayers and praises of Christian believers." Jails in every country have been home to God's people.

Finally, some would die. "Be faithful until death, and I will give you the crown of life" (v. 10b). Martyrdom was a definite possibility. Indeed Polycarp, a bishop in the church in Smyrna, became one of history's best-known martyrs.

What does Christ promise His people when they are expected to suffer for Him? Why could the church in Germany—and for that matter, the church in America today—take heart?

CHRIST IS PRESENT WITH THEM

"I know your tribulation," He said. The years 1933–45 in Germany were thoroughly known by Christ. We need to hear this word from our Savior afresh in each generation. He knows us personally and nationally, politically and ecclesiastically. He knows how we are at a loss for words at school-board meetings when the curriculum is discussed; He knows how hesitant we are to witness to our colleague at work. He knows we are intimidated by the media. He knows that we would rather remain silent so that we can pass a course at the university than share what we believe. *He knows.*

When Stephen was stoned as the first martyr, Christ was watching. Heaven opened to receive him. Christ knew when the stones flew; He knew when His servant was about to arrive. In every generation, the church has to remember that Christ knows.

If only we could see our suffering from the standpoint of heaven, how different it would look! As I watch movies of the Third Reich and see the adulation given to Hitler, I consider how different it would have been if Christians had seen their trials from the long-range point of view. The pastors who swore allegiance to Hitler, apart from a few exceptions, have died. How different it must look to them now!

CHRIST CONTROLS THEIR SUFFERING

The text says, "The devil is about to cast some of you into prison, that you may be tested, and you will have tribulation ten days." Christ has His hand on the thermostat when His people pass through the furnace of affliction. The prison term of these believers was not determined by happenstance but by Christ.

Contrary to some popular teaching today, we cannot always be free of attacks from Satan. Christ put those believers into Satan's hands! But Satan would be in Christ's hands. Niemöller was right when he said that God had allowed Satan to shake the German church to separate the wheat from the chaff.

Satan is given the authority to cause believers to suffer. The Christians at Smyrna were asked to endure their satanically inspired trial, but it would only last ten days. Whether it is a literal or symbolic period of time is not known; the point is that it lasts only as long as God wills that it last. Christ determines its beginning and end.

CHRIST HAS A PURPOSE IN OUR SUFFERING

All these things will happen, He says, "that you may be tested." Because we are so precious to Christ, no suffering is ever meaningless. When we see Christ, one of the gifts we will offer Him is faithfulness in the various trials of our faith, which is "more precious than gold" (1 Peter 1:7).

God gets glory when we suffer for His name's sake: "If you are reviled for the name of Christ, you are blessed, because the Spirit of glory and of God rests upon you. By no means let any of you suffer as a murderer, or thief, or evildoer, or a troublesome meddler; but if anyone suffers as a Christian, let him not feel ashamed, but in that name let him glorify God" (4:14–16).

CHRIST PROMISES ETERNAL REWARDS

"Be faithful until death, and I will give you the crown of life" (Revelation 2:10). Christ will make it all up to us. He will be there for us and with us.

Hitler asked the German nation to suffer with him, and the Third Reich would last for a thousand years. He was wrong, of course; his Reich lasted twelve years and six months. And as his days were coming to an end, he shrieked, "Everyone has deceived me! No one has told me the truth!" Perhaps it never occurred to him that he had not been exactly honest himself. The proud dictator finally came to the realization that he was mortal after all.

WE DON'T NEED TO LIVE THROUGH A HOLOCAUST TO BE HEROIC. WE JUST NEED TO BE ALL THAT GOD WANTS US TO BE EVERY SINGLE DAY.

In sharp contrast, Christ has the present and the future under His control. He could promise His followers a new life on the other side because He had no human limitations. He can promise us eternity, and He has the resources to keep His word.

CHRIST WILL PUNISH THE WICKED

In the midst of injustices the human heart cries out for a judge who will set the record straight. As you enter Buchenwald, the concentration camp just outside of Weimar, the sign on the gate reads, *Jedem des Seine* (To Each His Own). This was a parody of justice, as if those who entered were really getting what they deserved. As we know, those who entered got anything but justice.

Who will set the record straight? Who will finally bring justice to the events that took place in Buchenwald and, for that matter, the injustices on this hapless planet from its beginning? God will!

The apostle John writes, "And when He broke the fifth seal, I saw underneath the altar the souls of those who had been slain because of the word of God, and because of the testimony which they had maintained; and they cried out with a loud voice, saying, 'How long, O Lord, holy and true, wilt Thou refrain from judging and avenging our blood on those who dwell on the earth?'" (Revelation 6:9–10).

That cry will be answered. Justice will be meted out with such accuracy that we shall forever sing, "Great and marvelous are Thy works, O Lord God, the Almighty; righteous and true are Thy ways, Thou King of the nations" (Revelation 15:3).

Thus in the end the victims of the Holocaust shall be avenged; the church, both apostate and true, shall be judged by God; one at the judgment of the Great White Throne, the other at the Judgment Seat of Jesus Christ. Those who have come under the protection of Christ and His sacrifice on the cross shall be spared the divine wrath that shall be unleashed upon the earth.

Today God is calling us to suffer too. Not the suffering of the church in Germany (though that could become our lot someday), but the suffering that comes when we accept the lordship of Christ over all of life. *We don't need to live through a holocaust to be heroic. We just need to be all that God wants us to be every single day.*

Now we turn to a closer look at one of the heroes of the Nazi era. We will see that the strength of his faith can be ours too.

CHAPTER NINE

THE COST OF DISCIPLESHIP IN THE THIRD REICH

W hen God calls a man, he bids him come and die," wrote Dietrich Bonhoeffer during the dark days when the church in Germany was being "Nazified." He knew whereof he spoke. He followed Christ, and at the age of thirty-nine he died.

The life and death of Dietrich Bonhoeffer is an intriguing study in leadership, theological insight, and courage. The more I learn about him, the more I am forced to ask, What made him different? Why was he willing to stand alone when so many others did not have the inner resources to do what they knew was right? Certainly we must see Bonhoeffer's remarkable faith as a gift of God. And yet faith, if it is worthy of the word, must rest on a solid theological foundation. Bonhoeffer reminds us that if we can grasp who Christ is and what He demands, if we can see the present in light of eternity, suffering in this world is not only manageable but is to be expected.

Bonhoeffer excoriated the church of his day: "We Lutherans have gathered like eagles around the carcass of cheap grace, and there we have drunk the poison which has killed the life of following Christ." The church was weak because it had misunderstood grace.

Cheap grace is the deadly enemy of our Church. We are fighting today for costly grace. Cheap grace means grace sold on the market like cheapjack wares. The sacraments, the forgiveness of sin, and the consolations of religion are thrown away at cut prices. . . .

In such a Church the world finds a cheap covering for its sins; no contrition is required, still less any real desire to be delivered from sin. . . . Cheap grace means the justification of sin without the justification of the sinner . . . it is grace without discipleship, grace without the cross, grace without Jesus Christ, living and incarnate.[1]

Bonhoeffer saw what others were either unable to see or did not wish to see, namely, that following Christ involved much more than catechisms and rituals. To follow Him was to focus on the message of the Cross without shading the message to fit the political *zeitgeist* (spirit of the age). He was committed to the separation of church and state; he insisted on a Christianity that was independent of political interference.

This man who called the church back to its mission would eventually join (some would say mistakenly) a conspiracy to assassinate Hitler. Whatever we think of that decision, his heroism, zeal, and (from a human point of view) failure deserve careful consideration. At great personal cost he raised the flag of Christ, though most turned aside to follow another banner. *He did all he could to rescue the Cross from the swastika.*

THE LIFE OF BONHOEFFER

Bonhoeffer was born in Breslau in 1906, only thirty-five years after the beginning of the Second Reich when William I was crowned Kaiser Wilhelm in the palace of Versailles. Dietrich would have been twelve years of age when Germany was humiliated, having to admit defeat in World War I. The Kaiser, you will recall, was forced to abdicate, and the Weimar Republic was established.

Dietrich's father, Karl, was a professor of psychiatry and neurology at the university hospital in Breslau. But when Dietrich was six years of age, his family moved to Berlin where his father was appointed professor of psychiatry and nervous diseases in a Berlin hospital. This world-class city introduced Dietrich to cultural and intellectual pursuits. Though he would leave Berlin many times during his life, he always thought of the city as his home.

Dietrich Bonhoeffer in the courtyard of Tegel Prison the summer before his execution.

The Bonhoeffer family believed in Christian piety but did not attend church; they read the Bible but only on special occasions. Baptism and confirmation were important, but church attendance was seen as optional, unnecessary for a commitment to high ideals. Understandably, it came as a surprise to his family when Dietrich announced at age seventeen that he wished to study theology. Actually, the decision had already been made quietly in his mind before that, perhaps even when at the age of eight he and his twin sister spent time talking about death and eternity.

His oldest brother, Walter, was killed after his second week in combat during World War I. The Germans had been so confident of victory that when they were forced to accept defeat, the nation went into mourning. Dietrich's two surviving older brothers were convinced that Germany needed something more than theology to rescue it from its humiliation and political disarray.

Klaus, the oldest surviving brother, struggled to impress on his younger brother the feeble character of the Protestant church in Germany and grieved that Dietrich would give his life to such an irrelevant cause. To that, Dietrich stoutly replied, "If the Church is feeble, I shall reform it!"

His other brother, Karl, was even more unhappy about Dietrich's intentions. He spread out a map of the solar system, pointing out the latest discoveries of science. Karl was a confirmed skeptic and feared that his brother was about to give himself to a lost cause, a cause that was no longer relevant in a modern scientific age. But Dietrich would have none of it and replied, *"Dass es einen Gott gibt, dafür lass' ich mir den kopf abschlagen"* ("I shall believe God exists even if you knock my head off"). His determination to study theology remained unshaken.

Dietrich's parents showed little enthusiasm for their son's decision to study for Christian ministry. His mother was largely silent about the matter, and his father, believing a child should make his own decisions about a career, offered no opposition. But for the most part, the family saw the church as peripheral to the political and economic chaos that was then rampant. Changes that really counted would have to arise from elsewhere.

The Bonhoeffers were among the few families who supported the Weimar Republic, believing that only a democracy could guarantee individual freedoms. But when the terms of the Treaty of Versailles were announced a year later, the family, along with the rest of Germany, was angry at what they perceived to be burning injustice.

When inflation reached its peak in 1923 with a billion marks to a dollar, the family suffered. Germans spent their money the day they got it since inflation increased daily. Karl, the father, recounts that during this period two of his life insurance policies came due, each worth fifty thousand marks. He had promised the children that he would spend the money on a bottle of wine and some strawberries. In fact, the bottle of wine had to be abandoned—the insurance money paid only for the strawberries.

TRAINING FOR THE MINISTRY

Despite rampant inflation, Dietrich began the fulfillment of his dream and enrolled in Tübingen University in 1923. He studied there for only one year, concentrating on theology and church history. The next year he enrolled at the University of Berlin, continuing his studies in theology under the watchful eye of liberal scholars such as Adolf von Harnack. There Bonhoeffer was exposed to scholarship that undermined the historic Christian faith through critical research that insisted that the Bible was filled with errors and mythology. Popular discussions were held on the quest for the historical Jesus, that is, the real Jesus whom the liberals believed was nothing more than a remarkable man.

Bonhoeffer was impressed with such scholarship but never did accept the conclusions of these professors. He was friends with the Swiss theologian Karl Barth, who had himself abandoned the accepted liberal scholarship of the time and insisted that the church return to declaring "God to be God"; Barth preached that in Christ God was revealed as in no other. Unless the church returned to its task of preaching the gospel, it would have failed in its mission.

In this caldron of theological controversy, Bonhoeffer's interest in the role of the church in society was sharpened. At the age of twenty-seven, he published his dissertation entitled the "Communion of the Saints," which Karl Barth later called "a theological miracle." In it Bonhoeffer declared that the church is "Christ existing as community." The church, he said, is not a church, unless it "exists for others."

He agreed with Luther that the church was not an ideal society that was never in need of reform; rather, as a community it was capable of being untrue to the gospel. The church always has to return to Christ as the center.

We need to hear his passionate words for our own day: "There is only one hope for our age, which is so powerless, so feeble, so wretchedly slight and pitiable, and with all this so forlorn; return to the Church, to the place where one man bears up another in love, where one man shares the life of another, where there is fellowship in God, where there is home, where there is love."[2] As he had promised his brothers, he would reform the weak church.

EARLY MINISTRY

Since Bonhoeffer had not reached the minimum age for ordination, he accepted an appointment as an assistant pastor in Spain (1928–29). There he encountered poverty for the first time and helped organize a program to help the needy. He challenged his church: "God wanders among us in human form, speaking to us in those who cross our paths, be they stranger, beggar, sick, or even in those nearest to us in everyday life, becoming Christ's demand on our faith in Him."

When he returned to Germany, he was accepted as a professor at the Berlin University. This opened the door for a scholarship to Union Theological Seminary in New York. In America he became friends with such theologians as Reinhold Niebuhr, who challenged his thinking about social issues. He spent countless hours with black students who helped him understand the pain that racism caused in America. He frequently attended black worship services and took recordings of black spirituals back to Germany to play for his students. He also became a pacifist, believing that war was inherently contrary to the gospel. In battle, he believed, Christians killed one another for worldly political ideals, obscuring the weightier spiritual realities. While in America, he began to focus his study on the Sermon on the Mount.

GIVEN THE CONDITION OF THE CHURCH IN GERMANY IN THE 1920s, THE THEOLOGY OF BARTH AND BONHOEFFER WAS LIKE A COOL BREEZE IN A BURNING DESERT.

Bonhoeffer's exposure to liberalism both in Germany and later at Union Seminary has often made evangelicals in America skeptical of his theology. The fact that he did not condemn liberalism outright, and his own references to "a religionless Christianity," have left some evangelicals doubting his genuine commitment to the Christ of the New Testament. However—and this is important—Bonhoeffer went out of his way to insist that the Bible is the revelation from God, even though he was unable to answer all of the arguments of those who objected to such evangelical theology. Bonhoeffer went out of his way to insist that the Bible is the revelation from God, even when he was unable to answer all the arguments of those who tried to debunk evangelical theology.

"First of all, I confess quite simply," he wrote, "that I believe that the Bible alone is the answer to all of our questions, and that we need only to ask repeatedly and a little humbly, in order to receive this answer. . . . Only if we expect from it the ultimate answers, shall we receive it. That is because the Bible speaks to us."[3] And, at the center of the Bible's message was Christ and His cross. To a friend he wrote,

"My past is brimful of God's goodness and my sins are covered by the forgiving love of Christ crucified."[4]

Certainly we could wish that Bonhoeffer and his friend Karl Barth would have been more forthright in affirming the reliability of the Bible even in its historical details; we could wish that they had stood against the liberalism that was denying the very gospel Germany needed so desperately. But the fact remains that given the condition of the church in Germany in the 1920s, the theology of Barth and Bonhoeffer was like a cool breeze in a burning desert.

In America, Bonhoeffer said, he became a Christian, and for the first time in his life he was "on the right track." He meditated continually on Christ: "Faith is the experience of the concrete presence of Christ who was made flesh, crucified, and resurrected." He was deeply in love with Christ and willing to die that others might be ignited by the same flame. No one can read his writings without feeling his passion, his probing mind and heart.

STRUGGLES WITH THE CHURCH

After his return to Germany in 1931, Bonhoeffer continued his relentless quest to answer questions to which the German church needed answers. Hitler was beginning his ascent to power, and Bonhoeffer warned his students about German nationalism, which was derailing the true message of the church. All secular gods had to be renounced.

He was grieved by those students who chose to accept the popular ideology that what was good for Germany was good for the church. After Hitler became chancellor in 1933, Bonhoeffer was even more direct in his criticism of the Nazi regime and the failure of the church to stand against political interference. Bonhoeffer marveled at how easily people confused political success with spiritual success.

He kept asking his students, "Who is Jesus Christ in the world of 1933?" For him, Jesus Christ was the persecuted Jew and the imprisoned dissenter in the church struggle. When on April 1, 1933, a command was issued to boycott Jewish shops, the entire Bonhoeffer family disobeyed the order. Dietrich's ninety-year-old grandmother walked quietly through a cordon of SA men who were picketing the Jewish shops and made her purchases.

Bonhoeffer believed that the responsibility of the church went beyond its walls to all who were treated unjustly. As we have learned,

Boycott of Jewish shops in Berlin, 1933.

he opposed the Aryan Clause and wrote a paper in which he emphasized that membership in the church should be based not on race but
on one's relationship with Jesus Christ. He asked the church to defy
the state when its policies were on a collision course with Christianity.

He found himself increasingly isolated as a lecturer at the university. Amid the tide of rising Nazism, he was rejected for the pastorate. Frustrated, he left Germany in the fall of 1933 to accept the
pastorate of two German-speaking churches in London. He was
criticized by some, including Karl Barth, for abandoning the fight.
But Bonhoeffer used his foreign contacts to put pressure on the
German churches to resist the Nazified gospel.

In 1935 he returned to Germany to direct an illegal seminary
near the Baltic Sea. The seminary would refuse government support and hence be free from political interference. The intention
was to train pastors for the Confessing Church who would be free
from the theological errors of the "German Christians," who found
Nazism compatible with their own cherished beliefs.

At the seminary, Bonhoeffer structured the day around prayer, meditation, biblical readings, and his own lectures. Those lectures formed the basis of his most popular book, *The Cost of Discipleship*. Though the Gestapo closed the seminary in 1937, his legacy lives on through that book. He reminded those "German Christians" who united Christianity and National Socialism that "the cross was above the world. It means that man, even the noblest, must whether he likes it or not, fall in the dust and with him all gods and idols and lords of this world. The cross of Jesus Christ, that means the bitter scorn of God for all human heights, bitter suffering of God in all human depths, the rule of God over the whole world."[5]

Those who joined the Cross and the swastika were like those who made the golden calf in the Old Testament. The call to follow Christ meant that there was only one way to follow Christ and that was to leave all because "the road to faith passes through obedience to the call of Jesus."

On "Crystal Night," November 9, 1938, when the police watched passively as Jewish businesses were destroyed, synagogues burned, and Jews were imprisoned, Bonhoeffer returned to Berlin, furious with those Christians who said that it was simply the curse the Jews deserved because of the death of Christ. In his Bible he underlined Psalm 74:7–8: "They have burned Thy sanctuary to the ground; they have defiled the dwelling place of Thy name. . . . They have burned all the meeting places of God in the land." He condemned the dishonorable silence of the church and kept pressing the question, "Where is Abel your brother?"

The next year, 1939, Bonhoeffer returned to America to rethink his commitment to the Confessing Church and to remove himself as a symbol of church resistance. He believed that his continued presence would bring the wrath of the Nazis upon his closest colleagues. But troubled of conscience, he returned to Germany after just one month.

Before I describe how his life ended at the age of thirty-nine, let's answer this question: What did Bonhoeffer understand the cost of discipleship to be? And what did he mean when he said that Christ calls us to "come and die"?

COME AND DIE

If we ask why Bonhoeffer had the courage to be martyred, we can only answer that he died many times before he was hanged at the concentration camp in Flossenbürg. He was passionately convinced that discipleship meant death—death to our own comforts, death to our own agendas and, when necessary, physical death too. The cross of Christ was a symbol of that death and could never be confused with a swastika, which was a symbol of man's quest for life.

Bonhoeffer agreed with Luther that grace alone can save us, but those who followed him took up the doctrine, leaving out the resultant responsibility of discipleship. We are sustained in our suffering by realizing that God has been suffering through Christ in this world. God Himself was left cold and rejected; God Himself endured the humility of the cross. A mark of the true church is to be always suffering.

We follow Christ in His weakness that we might be strong. Christianity is a religion of suffering; a man throws himself into the arms of God and awakes in Gethsemane. If Christ died for what He believed, should not we follow in His footsteps?

Following Christ liberates us from all man-made dogmas, from every burden and oppression, from every anxiety and torture that afflicts the conscience. Only if we follow Christ unreservedly and single-mindedly do we find His yoke easy and His burden light. Thankfully, whatever Christ asks us to do, He gives us the strength to perform.

Here are five deaths the Christian must die—deaths that enabled Bonhoeffer to make the ultimate sacrifice with inner tranquillity and resignation to God. In some instances I quote Bonhoeffer; at other times I offer a paraphrase of his thoughts.

DEATH TO NATURAL RELATIONSHIPS

During the days of the Third Reich, many pastors said that they would be willing to endure imprisonment or death, but they could not do so because of their families. It is one thing for a husband/father to be persecuted; it is quite another to see children suffer a similar fate. Hitler always used a man's family as an inducement for absolute obedience.

Bonhoeffer answered that our commitment to Christ should be so all-consuming that all natural affection must come under its authority. "He who loves father or mother more than Me is not worthy of Me; and he who loves son or daughter more than Me is not worthy of Me" (Matthew 10:37).

Our break with natural relationships is sometimes external and sometimes hidden. But we must always be ready to let the breach come out into the open. Abraham had to leave his friends and relatives to follow God; nothing was to come between Abraham and his God. He had to become a stranger and sojourner to inherit the Promised Land.

Later God asked Abraham to offer Isaac on the altar as a test to see if the old man had allowed his son to worm his way into his heart. Could it be that Isaac meant more to him than God? No one else hears this call of God to Abraham, not even the servants or Sarah. It is God's personal call to him to hide nothing from the sovereign grace of the Almighty.

Abraham passed the test, and Bonhoeffer writes, "This time the direct relationship not only of flesh and blood, but also of the spirit must be broken. . . . Against every direct claim upon him, whether natural, ethical or religious, he will be obedient to the Word of God. . . . Abraham receives Isaac back, but henceforth he will have his son in quite a new way—through the Mediator and for the Mediator's sake."[6]

Abraham comes down from the mountain just as he had gone up, with his son at his side; but the whole situation had changed. Christ had stepped between Abraham and his son. "Outwardly the picture is unchanged, but the old has passed away, and behold all things are become new. Everything has to pass through Christ."[7]

Bonhoeffer knew whereof he spoke. He had not only left his family but the special love of his life, a young woman named Maria, to whom he was engaged. Three months after their announcement, Bonhoeffer was imprisoned. She was permitted to visit him in prison a number of times, and letters were smuggled in and out, sometimes with the cooperation of the guards. When he was moved to the Gestapo prison in another part of Berlin she was not permitted to see him again.

For Bonhoeffer his relationships were always subject to a higher obligation. We might think our first responsibility is to our families, our children, our boyfriend or girlfriend—we may believe that these relationships that have been established by God should never be broken. But Christ comes between us. He has a prior call.

DEATH TO SUCCESS

Ask the average Christian to measure success, and he will point to either wealth or power. Christ demolishes all such human notions.

Bonhoeffer said, "Success is a veneer that covers only the emptiness of the soul."

It is difficult to reprove a successful man for his behavior. For one thing, he is often unwilling to face up to his past since he is bent on his next achievement. He is propelled by a sense of his own importance, which will not be taken away from him. He is blind to his greed and ambition, since his success extols these attributes as good.

Second, he will rationalize his success by saying that he is doing it for God. Thus his own life and security become the nest within which he feels content and self-satisfied. He does not understand that it was that definition of success that crucified Christ. That understanding of success makes Christians indistinguishable from the world. How can we overcome the world if we have embraced its passion for success?

The Cross changes our perspective. Christ on the cross cannot be reconciled with our understanding of success. The Christian "is not concerned with success or failure, but with the willing acceptance of God's judgment."[8] We must lay our cherished dreams at the feet of our crucified Savior.

DEATH TO THE FLESH

What stands directly in our path as we seek to follow Christ more than the desires of the flesh? Those desires are deceptive.

To illustrate Bonhoeffer's point, I will add a story I heard from a fellow pastor who was discipling a group of men. Several of them confided to him that they would not accept victory over sexual lust even if Christ were to give it to them. Their argument was that lust is pleasurable, and given the pressures of life they deserved this bit of pleasure.

Bonhoeffer would say that those men have missed an important point: the need for faith, that God's way is actually best for them. When we turn our backs on Christ in this matter, we are unable to withstand the onslaught of temptation in other areas.

Here is Bonhoeffer's analysis: "Even momentary desire is a barrier to the following of Jesus, and brings the whole body into hell, making us sell our heavenly birthright for a mess of pottage and showing that we lack faith in him who will reward mortification with joy a hundred fold."

He goes on to expose the heart of the matter:

Instead of trusting to the unseen, we prefer the tangible fruits of desire, and so we fall from the path of discipleship and lose touch with Jesus. Lust is impure because it is unbelief and therefore is to be shunned. . . . The gain of lust is trivial compared with the loss it brings. . . . When you have made your eye the instrument of impurity, you cannot see God with it.[9]

Bonhoeffer speaks to our culture, which affirms that sexual pleasure is everyone's right. Some even think it is necessary, that it is simply a part of our humanity. But its power cannot be broken unless there is a definite decision to follow Christ, to look upon Him only. The Cross bids us come and die.

Self-will must be broken. We must become weak that we might become strong; Christ must come into every part of our lives. Bonhoeffer would agree with Tozer: "That part of us that we rescue from the cross becomes the seat of our struggles."

DEATH TO THE LOVE OF MONEY

"Do not lay up for yourselves treasures upon earth, where moth and rust destroy, and where thieves break in and steal. But lay up for yourselves treasures in heaven, where neither moth nor rust destroys, and where thieves do not break in or steal; for where your treasure is, there will your heart be also" (Matthew 6:19–21).

HE DECLARED THE CHURCH "GUILTY OF THE DEATHS OF THE WEAKEST AND MOST DEFENSELESS BROTHERS AND SISTERS OF JESUS CHRIST."

There are few people who are both wealthy and poor in spirit. The love for money must be offered up even as Isaac was offered on the altar. God knows, says Bonhoeffer, that the human heart craves treasure; and God wants us to have treasure. But He wants us to have that treasure in heaven. Earthly treasures fade, but a treasure in heaven lasts forever. "Our hearts have room for only one all-embracing devotion, and we can cling to only one Lord."

Bonhoeffer died to his natural love for money. He believed that money was to be used, not collected. What little he had was seen as a gift from God. The only money we will see again, he said, is that which we gave to help others.

Dying those deaths prepared him for his final sacrifice. He will be numbered among those who were willing to take a risk, thereby proving that "he loved not his life unto death."

BONHOEFFER'S MARTYRDOM

Though Bonhoeffer initially believed that the Sermon on the Mount taught pacifism, he eventually joined a conspiracy to assassinate Hitler. In defense of his action, he wrote to his co-conspirators, "We have for once learned to see the great events of world history from below, from the perspective of the outcast, the suspects, the maltreated, the powerless, the oppressed, the reviled—in short, from the perspective of those who suffer."[10] He believed that taking the risk of killing Hitler was to follow Christ who risked His life to defend the poor and the outcasts.

In point of fact, Bonhoeffer was recruited for espionage in 1940 by his brother-in-law Hans Dohnanyi, who was a deputy in the *Abwehr* (military intelligence). Dohnanyi conferred with Admiral Canaris, the head of the *Abwehr*, who by this point was deeply involved in the Resistance movement. Together they worked out a pretext for Bonhoeffer's membership: He could use his church contacts to help assess the political situation in other European countries and America.

Under cover, however, Bonhoeffer was carrying out quite a different mission, namely, contacting the Allies to seek terms of surrender should the assassination attempt succeed. He also worked on a daring plan to smuggle Jews out of Germany. Meanwhile, he found time to continue work on his book *Ethics,* in which he rebuked the church for not raising its voice on behalf of the victims. He declared the church "guilty of the deaths of the weakest and most defenseless brothers and sisters of Jesus Christ."

As might be expected, his decision to become a double agent has been frequently debated by theologians. Some have agreed with his political involvement; others have been unwilling to number him among Christian martyrs, insisting that he died for a political rather than a religious cause. Whatever the conclusion, one fact is inescapable: Bonhoeffer weighed his options and chose to risk his life for what he believed to be right.

On April 5, 1943, he was suspected of disloyalty and incarcerated in the Tegel military prison in Berlin. The evidence against him was vague, but he was held there and never again released. While in prison he wrote his book *Letters and Papers from Prison,* which was smuggled out by sympathetic guards.

He passionately attacked a form of religion that short-circuited genuine faith. He believed that often abstract theological debates obscured the answers that people desperately needed. The church, he said, was anxious to preserve its clerical privileges intact; it had jettisoned personal responsibility and failed to exercise authority over a "world come of age." *The church can only be the church if it acts courageously in a time of need.*

When Allied bombs damaged the prison, Bonhoeffer gave the other prisoners comfort. One inmate said that his commitment to Christ was evident and everyone was moved "by his simple sincerity."

On July 20, 1944, Colonel Stauffenberg's plot to assassinate Hitler failed. This precipitated the slaughter of many who were somehow believed to be connected with the conspiracy. Bonhoeffer was transferred to the Gestapo prison in Berlin in October of that year. In February 1945 he was taken to the concentration camp in Buchenwald. A fellow prisoner wrote of him, "He was one of the very few men I have ever met to whom his God was real and ever close to him." Another said, "Just quite calm and normal, perfectly at ease, his soul shone in the darkness of our prison. He learned to throw himself completely into the arms of God taking seriously his own suffering as well as the suffering of God in the world."

Two months later, by the order of Himmler, Bonhoeffer, along with Canaris and several others, was loaded into a prison van and taken to the extermination camp at Flossenbürg. A few days later they reached the tiny village of Schönberg, where the prisoners were herded into a small schoolhouse now used as a temporary lockup. One of the prisoners recounted that Bonhoeffer led them in a prayer service on the text "With his stripes we are healed," bringing comfort to his fellow prisoners.

The door was pushed open, and two members of the Gestapo entered, demanding that Bonhoeffer follow them. He took the time to bid everyone farewell. His last recorded words were, "O God, this is the end—for me, the beginning of life."

His mock trial continued through the night and into the morning hours. Our last picture of him comes from a description given by the doctor who was asked to witness the execution. He recorded that between five and six o'clock, Bonhoeffer and three others were led to their execution. The doctor said that when the door opened, he saw Pastor Bonhoeffer still in prison clothes praying to the Lord his God.

The prisoners were ordered to strip. Then they were led down a flight of steps under the trees to the secluded area of their execution. Naked under the scaffold in the sweet spring woods, Bonhoeffer knelt for the last time to pray. Then he climbed the steps to the gallows, brave and composed. Five minutes later, his life was ended, April 9, 1945.

Speaking of Bonhoeffer's faith, the doctor wrote, "The devotion and evident conviction of this man moved me to the depths. . . . In almost fifty years that I worked as a doctor, I have hardly ever seen a man die so entirely submissive to the will of God."

Three weeks later Hitler committed suicide, and a week after that the war in Europe ended. The Nazism against which Bonhoeffer stood was disgraced, and the church which he had so passionately judged was left to ponder its own failure of nerve. The message of the Cross that was lost during the heady days of national victories would have to be reclaimed.

If we ask why God did not spare Bonhoeffer's life for just a few more weeks so that he might be freed by the Allies, we cannot answer. We can only be certain that he died at God's appointed time and in God's appointed way. He who loved Christ with such fervency followed his Master in dying a violent death at the hands of others. He would say that God gave him the privilege of "costly grace."

Bonhoeffer's legacy lives. He is a constant reminder that the church must always remain the church, even at great personal cost. Christ invites all of us, "Come and die." But if we do not die to ourselves while our earthly life lasts, we will probably not be willing to pay the final price should our faith require it.

Bonhoeffer left behind a prayer: "Death, throw off our grievous chains and demolish the thick walls of our mortal body and our blinded soul, so that at last we may behold what we have failed to see in this place. Freedom, long we have sought you through discipline, through action and through suffering. Now that we are dying we see you there in the face of God."[11]

CHAPTER TEN

AMERICA'S OWN HIDDEN CROSS

Christianity in Germany bears a greater responsibility before God than the National Socialists, the SS and the Gestapo." So said Martin Niemöller during a lecture in Switzerland in 1946. If it is true that the strength of the church is determined by its impact in society, Niemöller just might have been right.

Germany and the United States have this in common: Both countries had Christian roots, a widespread acceptance of biblical social values, and a basic commitment to private virtue. America has benefited from the constitutional guarantee of the separation of church and state, and from democracy itself, a form of government that failed in Germany during the Weimar era but was finally adopted after World War II.

Despite the differences, the American church, like that of Nazi Germany, is in danger of wrapping the cross of Christ in some alien flag. There is evidence, I am sorry to say, that we evangelicals have lost our confidence in the gospel as "the power of God unto salvation." Luther reminded us that the church is a community that is in need of continual reform, always examining itself as to whether it is being true to Christ's mandate. I believe we must not only pray for revival but also for a reformation that will restore our lost confidence in the Cross.

What if—what if it is true to say about America as Heinrich Heine said about Germany—that only the cross of Christ was keeping us from powerful forces of brutality that, if unleashed, would cause the whole world to be astonished? Do we not already see such forces at work, with the escalation of crime, the moral collapse in our schools, and the destruction of our families?

Have we—I speak to those of us who are committed Christians—have we forgotten that God's power is more clearly seen in the message of the Cross than in any political or social plan we might devise? Might not our search for some antidote to our grievous ills be symptomatic of our lost confidence in the power of the gospel to change people from the inside out? Do we cling to the Cross with the deep conviction that it is not simply a *part* of our message to the world, but rightly understood it is the *whole* of it?

We have witnessed increasing hostility against Christianity from society in general and from state institutions in particular. The restraints of our Christian past are being cast aside with cynical arrogance. In an effort to be "relevant," we now face the temptation of being diverted from our mission and becoming involved doing what is *good* while bypassing what is *best*.

What, after all, is the meaning of the Cross about which we speak? Why should Christians "cling to the old rugged cross" as the old hymn reminds us to do? Surely, we might think we have outgrown such sentimentality. But it is exactly here that Christianity stands or falls; it is the meaning of the Cross that gives Christianity power.

The Cross is nothing less than the self-substitution of God for us. Because God chose to forgive sinful humans, He could only do so righteously; in the words of Charles E. Cranfield, He chose "to direct against his own very self in the person of his Son the full weight of that righteous wrath which they deserved."[1] God the Son paid the penalty for our sins to God the Father; thus "Salvation is of the Lord."

The struggle of the Reformation was nothing less than a struggle for the correct interpretation of the Cross. When Luther finally understood that on the cross Christ took upon Himself the iniquity of us all and that through faith alone sinners could be reconciled to God, he was, in his words, "reborn and entered the gates of paradise." Little wonder that the Cross was ever after the center of all of Luther's teachings. At the Cross all narcissism ends; all attempts to impress God cease, and optimism about mankind's ability to build a better world on its own vanishes.

The Christian cannot approach the Cross with cool detachment. The Cross exposes the futility of all our self-righteousness; it reminds us that we are sinners incapable of bringing about our own reconciliation with God. Christ died to save sinners, to reveal the love of God, and to conquer evil. Before this Cross we can only stand with bowed heads and broken spirits.

And herein comes the warning. P. T. Forsythe, when speaking of the Cross as the focal point of God's work for sinners, wrote, "If you move faith from that centre, you have driven *the* nail into the Church's coffin. The Church is then doomed to death, and it is only a matter of time when she shall expire."[2] The church can only live and breathe at the Cross; without it there is no life and no reason to exist.

Let me repeat Forsythe's warning: *Without the Cross we pound a nail into our coffin!*

OUR TWO DANGERS

In our desperate moment in history we face two dangers. The first is to say that we must retreat from our cultural and spiritual battles to be true to the supremacy of the Cross. This viewpoint is right in emphasizing that our primary mission is to preach the gospel, but it fails because we end up preaching to ourselves.

After the Scopes trial in America, fundamentalists for the most part retreated from art, public education, and politics. They felt uneasy about becoming involved in "worldly" pursuits. Like the church in Germany, many believed that there were two spheres, but they took this doctrine a step further and said that the Christian should spend all of his or her efforts within the "spiritual" sector. To move beyond it was to become too "secular," too preoccupied with that which will pass away. These older fundamentalists were right in holding to the centrality of the Christian message but wrong in teaching that the Christian faith could be lived in isolation from the culture and its institutions. *Thus the Cross, though exalted among the faithful, was hidden from the world.*

The second danger is that we become so overburdened with social/political agendas that our message is lost amid these cultural skirmishes. The church has always faced the temptation to modify the gospel or make it secondary to a given political, philosophical, or cultural agenda. When this happens, Christians have exposure to the culture, but the Cross does not. Again, it is hidden.

Jacques Ellul, in *The Subversion of Christianity,* wrote, "Each generation thinks it has finally discovered the truth. . . . Christianity becomes an empty bottle that successive cultures fill with all kinds of things."[3] Regrettably, the Christian bottle has been filled with many different agendas. Early in the history of the church, the Cross was obscured by sacramentalism, the idea that salvation was a grace given through the rituals of the church. Salvation was no longer a personal relationship with God, but was reduced to partnership with the ecclesiastical structure. The bottle was emptied and filled with liturgy that could never bring a soul to God. *The Cross became an ornament hung around the neck, not an instrument that changed the heart.*

Rationalism and humanism arose in the eighteenth century, the fruits of the Enlightenment. Religion, it insisted, must conform to our understanding. Whatever seemed contrary to our sensibilities was eliminated. Miracles, for example, were discounted as being out of sync with the enlightened cultural mind-set. The Unitarians argued that God was too good to send man to hell, and the Universalists believed man was too good to be sent there. The Cross became a symbol of sentimental love, not the means by which Christ shed His blood to reconcile men to God.

Today the bottle of Christianity is often filled with psychology. Since Freud, the need for a religious conversion has been eliminated. Secular psychology denies that man fell from some previous state of holiness. Since he has not fallen, he has no need to be picked up, at least not by God. Salvation is simply a matter of having a healthy self-image. The cross of Christ is a symbol of man's alienation from himself; a reminder that man must be reconciled to who he already is.

The New Age movement, in combining Christianity with any number of Eastern/occultic ideas, ignores the Cross altogether. At best it is a symbol of self-awareness, a reminder of our need to get in touch with the world beyond us. According to this movement, the Cross does not humiliate us; it exalts us.

Some political activists have filled the Christian bottle with a strategy for political reform. Salvation, it appears, is electing conservatives to national and local office. Important though this might be, we must always remember that God is neither Republican nor Democrat. When the Cross is wrapped in the flag of a political party, it is always

An air view of Berlin showing the destruction wreaked by Allied bombers.

distorted or diminished. Even for some who have experienced its power, the Cross has become an addendum to what is thought to be more pressing agendas.

We must be involved in the political process but also keep our distance, fighting evil and encouraging good wherever it is found. Ultimately the ballot box cannot save us; only God can. And the Cross is the centerpiece of His agenda.

Only when the Cross stands alone, unencumbered with other religions, philosophies, or political ideologies, does it retain its power. The cross of Luther had power to humble and save sinners; the cross in the swastika exalted and affirmed sinners. The one brought sinners into the kingdom of God; the other brought them into a crumbling *Reich*.

REMINISCENT OF HITLER'S GERMANY, "SILENT NIGHT" MUST BE REPLACED WITH "RUDOLPH THE RED-NOSED REINDEER," CHRISTMAS MUST BE RENAMED WINTER SOLSTICE, AND CHRIST MUST STAND ASIDE FOR SANTA CLAUS.

How then do we exalt the Cross and yet become involved in the cultural and social battles of our time? How can we avoid the mistake of the monastery as well as the mistake of the religious zealot who burns abortion clinics?

Before we answer the question of what our priorities should be, we need to reflect on some parallels between the church in Germany and our own cultural/political struggles. As always, at the eye of the storm is the age-old conflict between church and state. The freedom to freely preach the Cross is at stake.

THE CROSS AGAINST THE WORLD

Hitler became the dictator of a country that was, at least nominally, Christian. He was faced with the challenge of how to rid millions of people of their faith in God and Christ. Christianity was not exactly discarded, but it was replaced by his "positive Christianity," which could comfortably coexist with Nazism. Like many in America today, he believed that Christianity should surrender its uniqueness so that the Cross could be joined to other ideologies. He could not tolerate Christians who worshiped Christ exclusively, so he limited the free exercise of religious expression to an ever smaller spiritual sphere.

That was exactly the kind of control that the framers of the American Constitution tried to avoid. When they passed the First Amendment, "Congress shall make no law respecting the establishment of religion nor prohibiting the free exercise thereof," they thought they were protecting freedom of religion, guaranteeing that people could freely live out their faith. That phrase was understood to mean that (1) Congress (or the state) should not interfere with religious practices and (2) that a national church would not be established to which everyone would be obliged to belong.

In the hands of an elite group of reformers this amendment is now being turned on its head in a way that would make its original authors wince. Today our courts often interpret freedom *of* religion as freedom *from* religion. Rather than separating the church from state interference, the meaning now is that religious practices should be ousted from the state. Powerful forces are seeking to uproot every vestige of Christian influence, rewrite our history, and banish God from the public sector.

In our country every December, ACLU attorneys are on a search, ready to threaten any town or city that dares to display a Nativity scene and eager to silence schoolchildren who want to sing Christmas carols in a school pageant. The goal, of course, is to allow Christmas to be celebrated but without any expression of its meaning. Reminiscent of Hitler's Germany, "Silent Night" must be replaced with "Rudolph the Red-Nosed Reindeer," Christmas must be renamed Winter Solstice, and Christ must stand aside for Santa Claus.

Of course, the rights of other religions must be respected; we would agree that no one should be coerced into participating in Christmas celebrations. Regrettably, we are apparently unable to create an atmosphere where the student in a classroom can draw a picture of Christ without believing we have infringed upon another student's rights. In Fairfax, Virginia, the class of a ten-year-old girl painted Christmas scenes on its classroom windows. Yet this girl was asked to wash her picture off because it was a Nativity scene!

And just as Hitler had the textbooks of Germany rewritten to bring them into line with national socialism, so today our textbooks are being revised to delete our Christian heritage and to promote humanistic values. Thus secularism, once in motion, relentlessly moves across the landscape, seeking to crush religion at any cost.

If you speak to these political liberals, they will piously tell you that they do believe in freedom of religion; but the only way to be fair to all religions, they will say, is to banish religion completely from public life. This, of course, is the basic policy of all regimes that deny freedom of religion. Whether in China or Hitler's Germany, the premise is the same: Religion cannot be corporately practiced in those spheres belonging to the state. Once that premise is established, the next step is to expand the state's powers to encroach directly on the free practice of religion, even in the "spiritual sphere." Consider:

- In San Jose, California, the city council moved to ban a manger scene from a public square yet spent $500,000 of public funds to erect a statue to Quetzalcoatl, the Aztec god of human sacrifice.

- In Irmo, South Carolina, an honor student was told that her portrait of Jesus could not be displayed with other artwork because of its religious content.

- In Ladue, Missouri, a student group had to go to court to win the right to meet in school. They did not want to bring weapons or drugs into the school, only their Bibles.

- In Virginia a principal told a handicapped girl that she could not read her Bible on the bus since the vehicle belonged to the school district.

- In California a homosexual, fired from the church staff, sued based on discrimination. The fact that the church eventually won the lawsuit is of small comfort: that such a trial could even be held is a serious threat to religious freedom.

- In Shanahan, Nebraska, a judge upheld the right of U.S. West Communications to fire an employee, Christine Wilson, for wearing a pro-life button to work. The judge said that it would have caused undue hardship on the company to "reasonably accommodate the woman's religious observance or practice."

In 1941, a briefing was distributed by the Confessing Church that described the situation in Germany at the time. It pointed out that there was no Christian art at state exhibitions, the newspapers did not have articles on the Christian point of view, and "that the Church has something to say about questions which concern the German people is not even remotely considered."

Then the monograph makes a comment that sounds as if it were written about America in the 1990s: "The state excludes the church from everything which it considers as belonging to the political sphere. At the same time the church is expected to shrivel up into nothing."[4]

Parallels between Nazi Germany and America can be overdrawn, but only those who are blind to the realities around us can deny that that report from Hitler's Germany has ominous warnings for the United States today. The enemies of religion are not even content with banishing religion from the state while allowing freedom of religion in churches and synagogues. The goal is total control—the complete submission of the church to the arbitrary moral whims of the political establishment.

This intrusion of the courts into the spiritual sphere can be expected to continue. As America slides into paganism, pressure will be brought to bear on the church to perform homosexual marriages. Preaching against abortion, homosexuality, or other religions will be defined as "verbal violence." If social planners have their way, churches and Christian schools will have to hire homosexuals in the interest of fulfilling hiring quotas. New laws will be passed that restrict people from witnessing about Christ in the marketplace and even over the radio. A hostile state, if it cannot extinguish the message of the Cross, will nevertheless seek to suppress it.

Freedoms will also be restricted in the workplace. The Oregon Bureau of Labor filed charges against James Meltebeke, the owner of a painting business in Oregon, for inviting his employees to church and telling one couple that they were living in sin and would go to hell if they did not get married and go to church. The Bureau ruled that his comments created an "intimidating and offensive working environment." Incredibly, it said that proselytizing was a physical act that could be regulated by the state. Witnessing could be forbidden if found "in violation of important social duties and subversive of good order." Meltebeke had to pay a $3,000 fine and post a sign in his shop that regulated discrimination.[5]

Meltebeke's experience could become standard policy if the guidelines of the Equal Employment Opportunity Commission were to become federal law. As I write, opposition to this new law has prevented its passage in Congress. But if history repeats itself, its proponents will return when political conditions are more favorable. Freedoms will be taken away under the guise of bringing about a "religion-free workplace."

Even now employers can express their religious convictions only at "tremendous risk of liability and potential loss of business."[6] Some employers, fearful of these new guidelines, will not allow Christmas carols to be sung at their company Christmas parties. Religious symbols, such as crucifixes or Bibles, could be outlawed under new guidelines. In effect people will be told that when they walk into an office they must leave their most cherished beliefs behind. We can say, as did the Christians in Nazi Germany, "The church is expected to shrink into nothing."

Incredibly, those who want to uphold freedom are targeted as the ones who want to destroy it. In an article titled "New Right Wrongs" the Reverend Robert Meneilly mounts an attack on extremists and zealous religionists who have propagated "devilish acts and . . . awful persecutions . . . hate crimes and political chaos." James Dobson, who was the special target of the attack, points out that Meneilly was not referring to the militant Islamic *jihad,* nor I might add even to Adolf Hitler, but to Christians who have had the audacity to speak out about the great issues of our time.

Meneilly said that such Christians are a greater threat to democracy than the old threat of Communism. In effect, he insisted that Christians had no right to speak their mind about political or social matters. If they kept their ideas to themselves, it would be acceptable, but to speak them is *verboten.*[7]

In effect, liberal social planners want us to simply surrender, to promise to close our mouths, keeping our views to ourselves. It is reminiscent of the German woman standing in the rubble of her city near the end of World War II. When a British soldier passed by, she said to him bitterly, "None of this needed to happen if you had just surrendered in 1940!"

These attitudes are supported by a largely sympathetic media that is determined to change America into the secular state it believes the nation should be. This explains why, according to some polls, more than one-half of Americans believe that the religious right is to be feared as the force that will remove our freedoms. The fact that the so-called "Christian Right" is, for the most part, simply trying to maintain some of the past freedoms enjoyed by this nation is ignored. Liberals are never labeled the "Radical Liberal Left" but are touted as the guardians of our freedoms.

The goal of our new "guardians of liberty" is to make sure that if Christianity survives in America it will be scrubbed clean of its uniqueness. This is the American version of Hitler's "positive Christianity," which is compatible with any number of other religions and moral viewpoints. Those who believe that the cross of Christ demands their absolute loyalty will not be able to practice their faith freely. Richard Neuhaus points out that the reason is that some believe that the state is to be "denuded of religion and religion is to be tolerated only when it is hermetically sealed off in the private sphere of life."[8] Only when the Judeo-Christian tenets are ripped out of the hearts and minds of Western culture will the radical secularists be satisfied.

We do not know where all this will end. What we do know is that we have the high honor of representing Christ in the midst of this ideological megashift. Our challenge is to rise to this hour of incredible challenge and opportunity.

So how can we maintain the primacy of the Cross and yet live out our faith in the marketplace of ideas? What should the church be doing at a time when so many forces are trying to neutralize its influence and limit its freedoms?

THE CROSS EXALTED AND APPLIED

Now is the time to prioritize our efforts so that we will do the maximum amount of eternal good in the time we have left. At all costs we cannot let the influence of the church "shrink to nothing." Actually, throughout most of its two-thousand-year history, the church has had to suffer for its faith; yet we have been largely exempt from persecution in this country. With confidence in God we can face the future with joy and hope.

THE BLESSINGS AND DANGERS OF UNITY

Paul the apostle longed to hear a report that would assure him that the church in Philippi was "standing firm in one spirit, with one mind striving together for the faith of the gospel" (1:27). "The faith of the gospel" refers to those doctrines that center on Christ and His work for us. Paul knew that the word *faith* and the word *fight* were inseparably united.

This "striving together" for the purity of the gospel must always be our highest priority. If the gospel is our most cherished possession, it can never be compromised, even if our numbers should dwindle and our moral crusades collapse. Yes, there is strength in numbers, but not in numbers that would dilute the purity of the gospel message. When the Christian leaders in Germany thought that the Cross could be used to support an ideology that would reform their nation, the gospel was lost.

Unity among believers when defending the gospel is always necessary, especially when there is pressure to compromise. When the sixth synod of the Confessing Church decided that it was up to each pastor to choose whether or not he would take the oath of loyalty to Hitler, it handed the Führer a tremendous victory. *Individuals standing alone, no matter how courageously, cannot have the same impact as thousands, if not millions, of people standing together.*

There is also another kind of unity that has its risks and rewards. For years evangelicals have cooperated with a broad spectrum of religious groups to fight such scourges as abortion, pornography, and the imposition of special laws that favor homosexuals. They have worked together to form crisis pregnancy centers and provide food for the hungry. That work is of course commendable since, in a democracy, we must join forces with all those who hold to family values, regardless of their religious commitment or lack of it.

We can organize a moral crusade, raise a flag, and work with anyone who will salute it. But let us not be so naive as to think that this is America's great hope. Darkness can only be dispelled by light, and light comes through the gospel of God's grace. *Let us never forget that the world's greatest need is always to see Jesus, to understand why He alone can reconcile us to God.*

Even when we engage in our cultural and political battles, our primary objective should be that the world might see Christ. Yes, we can be grateful for our political and legal victories, but what have we won if people are not introduced to a Savior who can reconcile them to God? That does not mean that we preach a sermon every time we attend the PTA or help a young woman choose to give her unborn child life. It does mean, however, that we conduct ourselves in such a way that we have credibility in sharing the Good News.

And if the choice should be between winning our "cultural war" and maintaining our commitment to a pure gospel, we must let the cultural battles take second place so that the Cross gets a hearing in the hearts of men and women. Of course the choice is never that clear-cut, but we must remember that God did not put us on this earth to save America but to save Americans.

When eighteenth-century England was decadent, with alcoholism, the exploitation of children, and rampant immorality raging, God graciously sent a spiritual awakening through the preaching of George Whitefield and John Wesley. Some historians believe this revival spared the nation from a fate similar to the French Revolution.

While we pray and wait for a revival we can do nothing better than to revive our confidence in the power of the Cross to do what moral reform cannot. Let us remember that the reentry of evangelicals into politics is commendable, but it is not the answer; it is only a means to the answer. Whether evangelicals act as lawyers in a court of law, protesters in a pro-life demonstration, or politicians, every vocation is a bridge to witness to the saving grace of God in Christ.

LOOKING BEYOND OUR WALLS

Bonhoeffer argued that the church had a responsibility to all men, even those who were outside its walls. When he saw the Jews being persecuted, he saw them as Christ being persecuted. He believed that the church had the obligation of "jamming the spokes of the wheel" so that the state might not be able to do its ghastly deeds without a struggle. Even if the church should lose those battles, it is necessary that they be fought. We must not retreat into dishonorable silence. "So then, while we have opportunity, let us do good to all men, and especially to those who are of the household of the faith" (Galatians 6:10).

Who is Christ for *us* today? Certainly the unborn child, the abused child, the single mother, racial minorities. But Christ for me is also my wife, my children, and my neighbors. Each Christian must determine how he or she should be involved in helping others, but each person's involvement is not an option. If the cross of Christ is the greatest expression of God's love to the world, then those of us who follow Him must show our love to the world as well.

It is time that Christians become leaders in art, education, politics, and law. Let's not make the mistake of the German church and isolate the spiritual sphere from the political, social, and cultural world. Bonhoeffer was critical of the church when its only interest was self-preservation. We should be characterized by giving, not withholding.

Since we share this planet with all of humanity, we must reestablish leadership in all of those areas where Christians often led the way. Education, politics, and law—here is where we must gain credibility so that the world will listen to our message. The Cross should be seen wherever Christians are found.

PATRIOTISM AND CIVIL DISOBEDIENCE

We must support our government, but we must be ready to criticize it or even defy it when necessary. Patriotism is commendable when it is for a just cause. Every nation has the right to defend itself, the right to expect the government to do what is best for its citizens. However, if the German church has taught us the dangers of blind obedience to government, we must eschew the mindless philosophy "My country, right or wrong."

No human institution can take the place of God. We must all make up our own minds as to where we draw the line. Do we protest at abortion clinics? Do parents send their children to public school though they will be taught how to be immoral? Do Christian students fall in line with the university's "politically correct" policy?

Today in America the expression is still commonly heard "He's a fine Christian and a good citizen." Often throughout the history of the church those two accolades could not stand together. We, like the church in Germany, may yet have to decide between the two.

THE POWER OF GOOD DEEDS

Peter wrote, "Keep your behavior excellent among the Gentiles, so that in the thing in which they slander you as evildoers, they may on account of your good deeds, as they observe them, glorify God in the day of visitation" (1 Peter 2:12).

We can do little to rectify the public perception of Christianity as it is filtered through the secular media. We can't do anything about the fact that our image has been tarnished by the radicals among us. What *can* we do? There is only one answer. Every single Christian must become an activist, assuming the delicate task of taking a loving but firm stand on the issues, yet presenting spiritual healing to a society that is afflicted with a disease called sin.

John Q. Citizen will never be convinced of the credibility of the Christian faith until he becomes personally acquainted with someone who lives out the Christian life, applying its values to every situation.

The message of the Cross will not be received unless it is wrapped in the life of an authentic believer. The world must see our "good deeds" before they will listen to our "good words." Many Americans think they don't know anyone personally who is a born-again Christian. They don't know anyone who is pro-life and yet loves women who have had abortions. They think they haven't met anyone who is opposed to homosexual values yet loves homosexuals. They have never met anyone who would oppose an occult curriculum in the public schools and yet be a genuinely caring individual. In point of fact, they do likely know such a person, but he or she has remained silent for fear of being thought a fanatic or religious nut.

Remember, our goal must always be to gain a hearing among the cynics of our time who believe that God is irrelevant to this enlightened age.

PREPARATION FOR CONFLICT

Peter wrote, "But sanctify Christ as Lord in your hearts, always being ready to make a defense to everyone who asks you to give an account for the hope that is in you, yet with gentleness and reverence" (1 Peter 3:15).

Every believer must be able to give a rationale for his or her faith, defending the supremacy of Christ over all other alternatives. We can no longer think that being a Christian means simply coming to church, listening to messages, and singing hymns—important though these activities are. Christians must begin to realize that all the good arguments are on our side.

We must teach parents, teachers, nurses, bankers, and attorneys to stand for biblical values; we must not be ashamed of "coming out of the closet" and letting people know that not everyone is buying into the relativistic values of our disintegrating culture. Christians must network so that they can overcome the world's perception that the Bible is believed only by those whom the *Washington Post* described as "poor, uneducated and easy to command."

THE CROSS REMINDS US THAT THE BATTLE IS NOT SO MUCH BETWEEN CHURCH AND STATE AS IT IS WITHIN OUR OWN HEARTS.

America is an angry nation—angry because of the emotional distress caused by the breakup of the home; angry because of crime; angry because of a perceived betrayal by politicians; angry also because each side in the culture war sees the other as the enemy of all that America should stand for.

We need to heal rather than hurt; we need to unite rather than divide. We have to model reconciliation in our churches so that the world will see what a redeemed community looks like. We must defend the gospel, though not ourselves. No retaliation, no threats, no self-pity. Just endurance, patience, love.

HUMILITY AND PURITY

We must realize that our public effectiveness is largely based on our private relationship with God. The American church participates in many of the same sins as the world. Our passion for God is smothered, and our vision is marred. "Blessed are the pure in heart, for they shall see God," said Christ (Matthew 5:8).

When we come to the foot of the cross, it is there that we finally are broken; it is there that we learn to reach out to our confused and hurting world. The Cross breaks down the barrier between us and the whole human race. Then we will no longer see ourselves as fighting the ACLU, the media, or the politicians. We must rid ourselves of the mentality that says, in effect, "If we just cleared all of them out, all would be well." Not so. As Os Guinness said, the problem with this view is "that there is no problem in the wider culture that you cannot see in spades in the Christian Church. The rot is in us, and not simply out there. And Christians are making a great mistake by turning everything into culture wars. It's a much deeper crisis."9

At last we come to the heart of the matter: The Cross reminds us that the battle is not so much between church and state as it is within our own hearts. *If Christ has all of us, if the Cross stands above politics and the world as Bonhoeffer has reminded us, we shall overcome regardless of the cost.*

As Christians we can welcome an assault on our freedoms as long as we see this conflict as an opportunity to bear an authentic witness for Christ. Without trivializing the great horror of what took place in Germany, it is nevertheless a fact that without suffering we would never have heard of a Niemöller or a Bonhoeffer or a Corrie ten Boom, whose family hid Jews at great personal risk and who discovered that "there is no pit so deep but that God's grace is deeper still."

Nor would we have read about thousands of courageous pastors, mothers, and fathers who kept living for God at great personal cost without any visible compensation in this life. Without suffering, God would not have seen their faith, which to Him is "more precious than gold."

And in the final conflict, when the curtain falls on Earth's decisive *Götterdämmerung,* Christ will set the record straight. Those who were faithful to Him and His cross will be rewarded with "joy unspeakable and full of glory." All rival crosses will be exposed and judged, and every knee shall bow and "every tongue confess that Jesus Christ is Lord, to the glory of God the Father."

Until then, God is glorified by our steadfastness. If we suffer faithfully, the Cross will be exalted in the world. Bonhoeffer was right when he said that *it is before that Cross and not before us that the world trembles.*

Sola Gloria!

PHOTOGRAPH ACKNOWLEDGMENTS

NOTES

CHAPTER 1: WAITING FOR HITLER

1. William L. Shirer, *The Rise and Fall of the Third Reich* (New York: Simon & Schuster, 1960), 48.
2. Adolf Hitler, *Mein Kampf*, trans. Ralph Manheim (Boston: Houghton Mifflin, 1943), 161.
3. Quoted in Shirer, *Rise and Fall of the Third Reich*, 98.
4. Frau Forester Nietzsche, *The Life of Nietzsche* (New York: Sturgis & Walton, 1921), 2:656.
5. "The Gay Science," in *The Portable Nietzsche*, ed. Walter Kaufman (New York: Viking, 1954), 125.
6. Ravi Zacharias, *A Shattered Visage* (Brentwood, Tenn.: Wolgemuth & Hyatt, 1990), 22.
7. Shirer, *Rise and Fall of the Third Reich*, 111.
8. Victor Frankl, *The Doctor and the Soul: Introduction to Logotherapy* (New York: Knopf, 1982), xxi; quoted in Ravi Zacharias, *Can Man Live Without God?* (Dallas: Word, 1994), 25.
9. Shirer, *Rise and Fall of the Third Reich*, 226.
10. Gerald Suster, *Hitler: The Occult Messiah* (New York: St. Martin's, 1981), 135.

CHAPTER 2: GOD AND HITLER: WHO WAS IN CHARGE?

1. Adolf Hitler, *Mein Kampf*, trans. Ralph Manheim (Boston: Houghton Mifflin, 1943), 3.

2. William L. Shirer, *The Rise and Fall of the Third Reich* (New York: Simon & Schuster, 1960), 349.

3. Ronald Lewin, *Hitler's Mistakes* (New York: Quill, William Morrow, 1948), 15–16.

4. Trevor Ravenscroft, *The Spear of Destiny* (York Beach, Maine: Weiser, 1982), 95.

5. Wilhelm Busch, *Jesus Our Destiny* (Basel, Switzerland: Brunnen, 1992), 195–96.

6. Shirer, *Rise and Fall of the Third Reich,* 8.

7. Ibid., 77.

8. Ibid., 1056.

9. Ibid., 1069.

10. Robert G. Waite, *Adolf Hitler: The Psychopathic God* (New York: Basic Books, 1977), 17.

11. Benjamin Wirt Farley, *The Providence of God* (Grand Rapids: Baker, 1980), 31.

12. Hugh Ross, *Creation and the Cosmos* (Colorado Springs: NavPress, 1993), 47–48.

CHAPTER 3: THE RELIGION OF THE THIRD REICH: THEN AND NOW

1. Robert G. Waite, *Adolf Hitler: The Psychopathic God* (New York: Basic Books, 1977), 261.

2. Dusty Sklar, *Gods and Beasts: The Nazis and the Occult* (New York: Dorset, 1977), 23.

3. William L. Shirer, *The Rise and Fall of the Third Reich* (New York: Simon & Schuster, 1960), 44.

4. Trevor Ravenscroft, *The Spear of Destiny* (York Beach, Maine: Weiser, 1982), 91.

5. Ibid., 92.

6. Ibid., 176.

7. Sklar, *Gods and Beasts,* 54.

8. Waite, *Adolf Hitler,* 27.

9. Ibid., 29.

10. Sklar, *Gods and Beasts,* 53.

11. Waite, *Adolf Hitler,* xi.

12. Quoted in Ravenscroft, *Spear of Destiny,* 64.

13. Ibid., 9.

14. Ibid., 3.

15. Sklar, *Gods and Beasts,* 3.

16. Ibid., 72.

17. Quoted in David Hunt, *Peace, Prosperity and the Coming Holocaust* (Eugene, Oreg.: Harvest House, 1983), 128.

18. Gerald Suster, *Hitler: The Occult Messiah* (New York: St. Martin's, 1981), 77.

19. Quoted in Hunt, *Peace, Prosperity and the Coming Holocaust*, 141.

20. Ravenscroft, *Spear of Destiny*, 188.

21. Hunt, *Peace, Prosperity and the Coming Holocaust*, 131.

22. "A Global Ethic," 1993 Parliament of the World's Religions, 9.

23. Robert Van Kampen, *The Sign* (Wheaton, Ill.: Crossway, 1992), 209.

24. Quoted in Texe Marrs, *Mega Forces* (Austin, Tex.: Living Faith, 1988), 24.

CHAPTER 4: THE ANTI-SEMITISM OF THE THIRD REICH

1. Trevor Ravenscroft, *The Spear of Destiny* (York Beach, Maine: Weiser, 1982), 251.

2. Ibid., 29–30.

3. Quoted in Kevin Abrams, "The Lambda Report," August 1994, 8.

4. Ibid., 9.

5. Martin Luther, *Luther's Works*, trans. Martin H. Bertram (Philadelphia: Muhlenberg, 1962), 47:268–72.

6. Ibid., 45:229.

7. Quoted in Ravenscroft, *Spear of Destiny*, 116.

8. Ibid.

9. Ibid., 147.

10. Dusty Sklar, *Gods and Beasts: The Nazis and the Occult* (New York: Dorset, 1977), 91.

11. Ibid., 151–53.

12. George M. Kren and Leon Rappoport, *The Holocaust and the Crisis of Human Behavior* (New York: Holmes & Meier, 1980), 70.

13. Ravenscroft, *Spear of Destiny*, 251.

14. Sklar, *Gods and Beasts*, 91.

15. Johannes Aagaard, "Hindu Scholars, Germany and the Third Reich," in *Update* (September 1982).

16. Curt Young, *The Least of These* (Chicago: Moody, 1983), 7–8.

17. David A. Rausch, *A Legacy of Hatred* (Chicago: Moody, 1984), 168.

CHAPTER 5: THE CHURCH IS DECEIVED

1. Eberhard Bethge, *Dietrich Bonhoeffer* (New York: Harper & Row, 1970), 191.

2. Richard Pierard, "Radical Resistance," *Christian History* 10, no. 4 (1991): 30.

3. J. S. Conway, *The Nazi Persecution of the Churches 1933–1945* (New York: Basic Books, 1968), 48.

4. Robert G. Waite, *Adolf Hitler: The Psychopathic God* (New York: Basic Books, 1977), 317.

5. Ibid., 16.

6. Richard Grunberger, *The 12-Year Reich* (New York: Holt, Reinhart & Winston, 1971), 439.

7. John Toland, *Hitler: The Pictorial Documentary of His Life* (New York: Doubleday, 1978), 47.

8. Oswald J. Smith, "My Visit to Germany," *The Defender* 11 (September 1936): 15; quoted in David A. Rausch, *A Legacy of Hatred* (Chicago: Moody, 1984), 101.

9. James Dobson in a letter to his supporters, March 1993.

10. William L. Shirer, *The Rise and Fall of the Third Reich* (New York: Simon & Schuster, 1960), 234.

11. Conway, *Nazi Persecution of the Churches*, 15.

12. Shirer, *Rise and Fall of the Third Reich*, 249.

13. Ibid., 241.

14. Ibid., 268.

15. Rausas J. Rushdoony, *Law and Liberty* (Fairfax, Va.: Thoburn, 1971), 73.

16. Shirer, *Rise and Fall of the Third Reich*, 238.

17. Ibid., 240.

18. Quoted in John Warwick Montgomery, *The Law Above the Law* (Minneapolis: Bethany, 1975), 25–26.

CHAPTER 6: THE CHURCH IS DIVIDED

1. Eberhard Bethge, *Dietrich Bonhoeffer* (New York: Harper & Row, 1970), 228.

2. Mary Bosanquet, *The Life and Death of Dietrich Bonhoeffer* (London: Hodder & Stoughton, 1968), 121–22.

3. Geffrey B. Kelly, "The Life and Death of a Modern Martyr," *Christian History* 10, no. 4 (1991): 11.

4. Bethge, *Dietrich Bonhoeffer*, 232.

5. Ibid., 241.

6. Kelly, "The Life and Death of a Modern Martyr," 13.

7. Peter Matheson, ed., *The Third Reich and the Christian Churches* (Grand Rapids: Eerdmans, 1981), 39–40.

8. Dietmar Schmidt, *Pastor Niemöller* (New York: Doubleday, 1959), 94. This helpful biography is the source of the story of Niemöller's meeting with Hitler.

9. Schmidt, *Pastor Niemöller*, 96.

10. Ibid., 97.

11. Arthur C. Cochrane, *The Church's Confession Under Hitler* (Philadelphia: Westminster, 1962), 14.

12. Barmen Confession; quoted in Matheson, ed., *The Third Reich and the Christian Churches*, 46.

13. Bosanquet, *Life and Death of Dietrich Bonhoeffer*, 163.

14. Matheson, *Third Reich and the Christian Churches*, 50.

15. Bosanquet, *Life and Death of Dietrich Bonhoeffer,* 165.

16. J. S. Conway, *The Nazi Persecution of the Churches 1933–1945* (New York: Basic Books, 1968), 377.

17. Dietrich Bonhoeffer, *Ethics* (New York: Collier Books, 1963), 65.

CHAPTER 7: THE CHURCH IS DISMEMBERED

1. Quoted in J. S. Conway, *The Nazi Persecution of the Churches 1933–1945* (New York: Basic Books, 1968), on an opening unnumbered page.

2. Mary Bosanquet, *The Life and Death of Dietrich Bonhoeffer* (London: Hodder & Stoughton, 1968), 166.

3. Peter Matheson, ed., *The Third Reich and the Christian Churches* (Grand Rapids: Eerdmans, 1981), 58–60.

4. William L. Shirer, *The Rise and Fall of the Third Reich* (New York: Simon & Schuster, 1960), 239.

5. Dietmar Schmidt, *Pastor Niemöller* (New York: Doubleday, 1959), 110–11.

6. F. Burton Nelson, "Family, Friends & Co-conspirators," *Christian History* 10, no. 4 (1991): 20.

7. Eberhard Bethge, *Dietrich Bonhoeffer* (New York: Harper & Row, 1970), 504.

8. Conway, *Nazi Persecution of the Churches,* 223.

9. Ibid., 220.

10. Shirer, *The Rise and Fall of the Third Reich,* 240.

11. Quoted in David A. Rausch, *A Legacy of Hatred* (Chicago: Moody, 1984), 169.

12. Conway, *Nazi Persecution of the Churches,* 87.

13. Helmut Thielicke, "The Great Temptation," *Christianity Today,* 12 July 1985, 24–31. My summary of the message is taken from this longer version.

CHAPTER 8: HEROISM IN THE THIRD REICH

1. Cited in Arthur. C. Cochrane, *The Church's Confession Under Hitler* (Philadelphia: Westminster, 1962), 40.

2. Ibid., 41.

3. Cited in Eberhard Bethge, *Bonhoeffer: Exile and Martyr* (New York: Seabury, 1975), 155.

4. Ibid.

5. Tim Stafford, "Campus Christians and the New Thought Police," *Christianity Today,* 10 February 1992, 19.

6. Roger Manvell and Heinrich Fraenkel, *The Men Who Tried to Kill Hitler* (New York: Coward-McCann, 1964), 209–11.

7. Ibid., 177–80.

8. Helmut Gollwitzer, Kathe Kuhn, and Reinhold Schneider, eds., *Dying We Live* (New York: Pantheon Books Inc., 1966), 162.

9. Bethge, *Bonhoeffer,* 156–58.

10. Bea Stadtler, *The Holocaust: A History of Courage and Resistance* (West Orange, N.J.: Behrman House, 1974). The book is filled with stories of the resistance; I allude here to only a few.

11. David P. Gushee, "Why They Helped the Jews," *Christianity Today*, 24 October 1994, 32–35. I've included a summary of his conclusions.

CHAPTER 9: THE COST OF DISCIPLESHIP IN THE THIRD REICH

1. Dietrich Bonhoeffer, *The Cost of Discipleship*, trans. C. Kaiser (New York: Macmillan, 1949), 45–46.

2. Mary Bosanquet, *The Life and Death of Dietrich Bonhoeffer* (London: Hodder & Stoughton, 1968), 65.

3. Ibid., 109.

4. Geffrey B. Kelly and F. Burton Nelson, eds., *A Testament to Freedom* (San Francisco: Essential Writings of Dietrich Bonhoeffer, 1990), 538.

5. Bosanquet, *Life and Death of Dietrich Bonhoeffer*, 121.

6. Bonhoeffer, *Cost of Discipleship*, 111.

7. Ibid., 112.

8. Dietrich Bonhoeffer, *Ethics*, trans. Neville Horton Smith (New York: Collier Books, 1949), 77.

9. Bonhoeffer, *Cost of Discipleship*, 148.

10. Geffrey B. Kelly, "The Life and Death of a Modern Martyr," *Christian History* 10, no. 4 (1991): 8.

11. Roger Manvell and Heinrich Fraenkel, *The Men Who Tried to Kill Hitler* (New York: Coward-McCann, 1964), 220–21.

CHAPTER 10: AMERICA'S OWN HIDDEN CROSS

1. Quoted in John Stott, *The Cross of Christ* (Downer's Grove, Ill.: InterVarsity, 1986), 134.

2. Ibid., 44.

3. Jacques Ellul, *The Subversion of Christianity* (Grand Rapids: Eerdmans, 1986), 18.

4. Peter Matheson, ed., *The Third Reich and the Christian Churches* (Grand Rapids: Eerdmans, 1981), 94–95.

5. Nicholas P. Miller, "Religion Free Workplaces?" *Liberty* (December 1984): 12–15.

6. Ibid.

7. James Dobson, "Freezing the Linebacker," *Liberty* (October 1994): 14–17.

8. Richard Neuhaus, National Federation of Decency, August 1987, 3.

9. As quoted in "Religion & Politics: A Round Table Discussion," *Modern Reformation* (September/October 1994): 25.

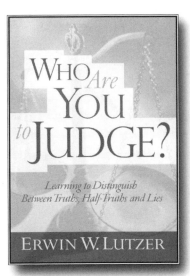